HEAR #METOO IN INDIA

HEAR #METOO IN INDIA

News, Social Media, and Anti-Rape and Sexual Harassment Activism

PALLAVI GUHA

RUTGERS UNIVERSITY PRESS
New Brunswick, Camden, and Newark, New Jersey, and London

Names: Guha, Pallavi, author.
Title: Hear #metoo in India : news, social media, and anti-rape and sexual harassment activism / Pallavi Guha
Description: New Brunswick, New Jersey : Rutgers University Press, 2021. | Includes bibliographical references and index.
Identifiers: LCCN 2020020797 | ISBN 9781978805729 (paperback) | ISBN 9781978805736 (cloth) | ISBN 9781978805743 (epub) | ISBN 9781978805750 (mobi) | ISBN 9781978805767 (pdf)
Subjects: LCSH: Rape victims—India. | Sexual harassment—India. | Sexual abuse victims—India. | Women—Violence against—India. | Women—Political activity—India. | Feminism—India.
Classification: LCC HV6569.I4 G84 2021 | DDC 362.8830954—dc23
LC record available at https://lccn.loc.gov/2020020797

A British Cataloging-in-Publication record for this book is available from the British Library.

Copyright © 2021 by Pallavi Guha
All rights reserved

No part of this book may be reproduced or utilized in any form or by any means, electronic or mechanical, or by any information storage and retrieval system, without written permission from the publisher. Please contact Rutgers University Press, 106 Somerset Street, New Brunswick, NJ 08901. The only exception to this prohibition is "fair use" as defined by U.S. copyright law.

♾ The paper used in this publication meets the requirements of the American National Standard for Information Sciences—Permanence of Paper for Printed Library Materials, ANSI Z39.48-1992.

www.rutgersuniversitypress.org

Manufactured in the United States of America

I dedicate this book to all the feminist activists and journalists who have given up comfort and pleasure to steadfastly work for the life and respect of the sexually abused and assaulted in India.

সুখের বদলে সম্মান বিকাইয়া দেওয়া যায় না। সুখ বিদায় হোক—সম্মান থাক জীবনে।
(We cannot compromise respect for comfort, let there be respect instead
of comfort in life.)

—Ashapoorna Devi (1909–1995), অগ্নিপরীক্ষা
(Ordeal to prove innocence)

CONTENTS

1	Introduction and Historical Background	1
2	Framing of Rape in the News Media and Its Impact on Feminist Activism and Journalists: #MeTooIndia Including Themes	23
3	The Heart Does Not Bleed for Everyone: Selective Outrage and Activism	46
4	The Successes and Failures of Transnational Hashtag Movements	59
5	Moving Forward: Learning from Anti-rape Feminist Movements	97
	Acknowledgments	115
	Notes	117
	References	119
	Index	135

HEAR #METOO IN INDIA

1 · INTRODUCTION AND HISTORICAL BACKGROUND

As a young girl and as a woman, one of my greatest fears has been sexual assault. Strangely, it is not the fear of death or of being hurt, but sexual abuse and assault. And now that I am the mother of a young girl, it is my greatest fear. However, when I read the testimonies of sexual assault survivors and victims and speak with them about their ordeals, I realize how little I am aware of from reading newspapers and social media. While doing the research for this book, I recalled the horrors of my own experiences of sexual harassment and street harassment, starting in my pre-teen years. Since then, I have learned to be cautious and have steadfastly followed the rules for "how not to be sexually abused or raped." I do not remember ever having any conversations about the perpetrators who engaged in rape and sexual abuse, about the public curiosity, or about the news media reporting, which centered on blaming or pitying the victim or survivor. Like many women in India, I experienced sexual harassment countless times but was at a loss as to how to react. Other than reprimanding the offender, I have done little; there were no social media platforms at that time to publicize incidents, and media reporting on sexual harassment and rape was limited. Years passed, and I realized that rape, sexual harassment, and violence unfortunately still remain relevant in various forms. We read about rape, sexual abuse, and sexual harassment happening within the family, in public spaces, in academic institutions, and in workplaces. Some rapes, sexual abuse, and sexual harassment incidents find space in the news media, some are discussed only on social media, and many do not reach the public at all. There is no denying that the news media coverage of and social media conversations about rape and sexual harassment have changed, but even today rape and sexual harassment victims and survivors are still questioned and blamed for sexual assault across societies and cultures. Despite the #MeToo and #MeTooIndia movements, many of those accused continue to thrive in their careers, even with proof of their misconduct and harassment. Following the same pattern of victim blaming, the motives of survivors and the initiators of #MeTooIndia have also been called into question.

The treatment meted out to rape and sexual assault victims and survivors has not been much different globally. From the heinous rape of women working on American farms to low-caste and low-class women in rural India, sexual assault and rape victims, survivors, and activists have sometimes mustered the courage to speak up, but it has not been easy; some have been failed by both the news media and social media platforms, and their voices have not reached the public. I do not claim to be the voice of these fearless women and activists, but through this book I share my conversations with anti-rape and sexual harassment activists and journalists engaged in public and political discourse on anti-rape activism.

In the course of writing this book, every time I decided to stop analyzing the news coverage of rape and sexual assault, there was yet another rape and sexual assault that made headlines, which changed the course of my writing. Finally, I decided to stop analyzing news coverage in July 2019, when, during one of our conversations, Sutapa, an anti-rape activist, said, "The ones that make the news are just the tip of the iceberg. There are so many sexual assaults that happen regularly in rural areas; can you take all of them into account?"

A SHIFT IN THE MEDIA LANDSCAPE

With the growth of digital communication platforms, feminist activists have become increasingly vocal about harassment and abuse globally, and the Google visualization of the #MeToo campaign provides an overview of its global reach. Over the past two decades, communication and technologies have evolved dynamically. The introduction and rise of the internet, political blogs, and social media networks have changed the media landscape, as well as the relationships between the different forms of media (Bekkers, Beunders, Edwards, & Moody, 2011). The internet and specifically the various social media networks have emerged as a global platform for transnational feminist activism (Munro, 2013; Schuster, 2013). Early online feminist activism resulted in campaigns such as SlutWalk, Pink Chaddi (Pink Underwear), and Hollaback, and more recent campaigns include #IwillGoOut, Pinjra Tod (Break the Cage), #LoSHA, and #MeToo.

According to feminist media scholars (Bianco, 2017; Crossley, 2015; Munro, 2013), the internet and social media platforms are emerging as a vital space for feminist activism. Feminist movements are mobilized on social media sites such as Facebook and Twitter, which can culminate in social movements (Crossley, 2015). However, the internet and social media platforms have also become spaces on which feminist activists are vulnerable due to trolling, doxing, and other forms of cyberharassment (Hess, 2014). According to a study conducted by the Broadband Commission Working Group on Gender in 2015, 73 percent of women have been victims of online hate and violence. In 2019, Amnesty International conducted a similar study and found that women still experience widespread harassment on Twitter: in an analysis of 14.5 million tweets mentioning women, around a million tweets were abusive toward women (as cited in Martin and O'Carroll, 2019).

Crossley (2015), Munro (2013), Schuster (2013), and others have focused their research on online feminist activism in America and Western European countries, where internet penetration and literacy are far higher than in emerging Asian economies such as India, China, and the Philippines. Although scholars are hailing social media platforms as spaces for marginalized groups, the trend of perpetuating online hate and violence against women is universal (Broadband Commission Working Group on Gender, 2015; National Public Radio, 2019).

Online feminist movements have increased in the past five years and now include the #WomensMarch, #TimesUp, and the #MeToo movement. Social media activism against sexual harassment in the recent past, including the #MeToo movement, has been an organic process. However, media activism against rape and sexual harassment is not new; it has been on the public and media agendas since the second wave of feminism in the 1970s (Mendes, 2011). While the second wave of feminism was primarily related to the feminist movement in the United States, feminists in India also spearheaded a movement to bring about reform of the existing rape and sexual harassment laws in the 1970s. This was made possible in large part by coverage of the activism in the news media and its agenda-building ability.

The anti-rape and sexual assault movement in the United States started in the 1970s, during the second wave of feminist activism. In India, the growing focus on rape and sexual assault of women in the 1970s and 1980s was driven at least in part by the infamous rape case in which Mathura, a tribal teenage girl, was gang-raped inside a police station by more than three police officers (Katzenstein, 1989; Patel & Khajuria, 2016). After eight years of legal deliberation, the Supreme Court of India (the highest court in India) stated in its judgment that Mathura had not been raped but had consented to have sex with the men (Neupane, 2014; Patel & Khajuria, 2016). Feminist activists protested against the decision to exonerate the police officers, and the movement demanded a review of the judgment in the Mathura case. This forced the Indian government to amend India's existing rape laws, which had previously put the burden of proof on the victim (I. Nagar, 2016; Patel & Khajuria, 2016).

Feminist activists also protested against the rapes of Rameeza Bee of Hyderabad and Maya Tyagi of Delhi, which also occurred while they were in police custody (Katzenstein, 1989). The amendment of the rape laws was a watershed moment for Indian feminist activism. Thus, the Mathura anti-rape activism consolidated the feminist movement in India and also amended the existing rape laws.

In 1992, Bhanwari Devi, a lower-caste grassroots government worker in rural Rajasthan, was raped in the course of doing her work of preventing child marriage.

Bhanwari Devi filed a case that led the Supreme Court of India to create sexual harassment guidelines for the workplace in India (Pandey, 2017). Unfortunately, Bhanwari Devi's upper-caste rapists were acquitted of rape and convicted on lesser charges (Pandey, 2017). There were no social media sites, internet, or hashtag activism when Bhanwari Devi was raped; her rapists were given much lighter sentences, and only the local media reported her struggles. After the #MeToo and #MeTooIndia movements started in 2017 and 2018, respectively, there was renewed interest in Bhanwari Devi's case, and several news media organizations interviewed her and wrote about her (Bhandare, 2019; Pandey, 2017; Sushmita, 2018). In one interview, Bhanwari Devi recounted the harassment from the police and the judiciary, including the refusal by the police to file her complaint and needing to give testimony eight times in twenty-six years (Sushmita, 2018). Indeed, Bhanwari Devi did not receive justice, but due to her filing the case, the Visakha Guidelines for sexual harassment policies at workplaces in India were eventually implemented (Pandey, 2017).

Bhanwari Devi's rape in 1992, Jyoti Singh's rape and murder in 2012, and the #MeToo movement in India have been called turning points in the Indian feminist movement (Bhandare, 2019).[1] Yes, they have brought the discourse on rape and sexual harassment to the forefront, but there is a clear lack of inclusivity with respect to whose stories are heard and amplified and whose remain unheard.

Few Indian women are strangers to sexual harassment, molestation, and other sex crimes (R. Guha, 2015; Singh, 2016). Although women are now more visible in public spaces, they continue to be harassed and violated (P. Guha, 2015; Nair, 2017). In 2013, the Justice Verma Commission was constituted after the infamous gang rape of Jyoti Singh in New Delhi on December 16, 2012. Changes were made to Indian rape law on the recommendation of the Justice Verma Commission, such as allowing the victims to file an online First Information Report (FIR), setting up rape crisis centers, ensuring that police help the victims irrespective of their jurisdiction, and more. After the #MeTooIndia movement in 2018, Maneka Gandhi, the minister of women and child development of India, proposed the formation of a judicial panel to look into the claims and issues of sexual harassment at the workplace (PTI, 2018). However, nothing concrete happened beyond the announcement of the panel, and in June 2019 it was quietly disbanded without any recommendations ("Govt Dissolves #MeToo Panel Quietly," 2019).

In the recent past, scholars and activists have hailed the role of social media platforms in anti-rape activism, but the role of news media platforms has been muted in this discussion. It is true that social media platforms provide an alternate space for activism, but in a country like India—one of the few countries that have a thriving circulation of print newspapers—the news media cannot be neglected (Audit Bureau of Circulation, 2017). According to a report published in May 2017 by the Audit Bureau of Circulation in India, the average daily circulation of newspapers increased by 4.8 percent over the previous decade. The value of printed material in India and the fact that reading the newspaper is part of the daily routine make newspapers accessible and relevant in India. The newspaper business in India is still the most influential print newspaper industry in the world (Bhargavi, Guru, & Joseph 2015; Kilman, 2015a).

The Indian print news media hold tremendous clout in acting as gatekeepers of the news, and they can play a crucial role in the formation of public opinion and public policy. Compared with other media platforms, print news media are known to provide in-depth coverage of policy-related issues (Manjappa, 2014; Ram, 2016). Hence, it would be premature to neglect the role of the news media in anti-rape activism completely. Historically, too, the Indian press has been involved in advocacy; it has been an essential tool for championing social, economic, and political issues, beginning with the Indian independence movement through the Chipko movement to the anti-corruption movement, and, most recently, the farmers' movement in India. Judging from the history of this relationship between the Indian press and social activism, I assumed that journalists and anti-rape and sexual harassment feminist activists would collaborate more to create an anti-rape and sexual assault agenda in India.

In the 1970s, violence against women became the cornerstone of feminist activism in India, resulting in increased coverage of this issue in Indian newspapers (D'Souza, 2009; Katzenstein, 1989; Neupane, 2014). Since independence, the Indian media have been responsible for both positive developments, such as the creation of employment opportunities and technological advancements, and adverse developments, such as the corporatization of the profession, leading to paid news, corruption, and gender-biased framing of issues (Ray, 1999). Chaudhuri (2000) observes that "representations of feminism in the print media surveyed are therefore replete with terms like 'unnatural,' 'excessive,' 'irrational,' and 'berserk'" (p. 273). This has led to further stigmatization of anti-rape and sexual harassment activists. The patriarchal, discriminatory view of women as the lesser sex, the lack of police and judicial support for assaulted women, and the general contempt for women's liberation create a view of feminism based on misunderstandings (Himabindu, Arora, & Prashanth, 2014; Shenomics, 2016). These range from feminists being man-hating, sex-hating, and depraved individuals to being angry bra burners (Madhok, 2015). Feminist activists are also infamously known as "feminazis" (Shenomics, 2016; Thomas, 2006).

The news media in many countries, including India, are legally bound to withhold the name of a woman who has been assaulted, in order to protect her honor. This is because rape not only stigmatizes but also objectifies the body of the woman. "The stigma associated with rape remains grave for rape victims and all too often impedes victims coming forward. Therefore, the cases that do come forward in the legal system tend to be the same sort of cases that the media deem . . . newsworthy. Moreover, these are most frequently the more unusual

6   HEAR #METOO IN INDIA

and the more sensational types of rape cases" (Ardovini-Brooker & Caringella-Macdonald, 2002, p. 4), which is true globally. Rape and sexual assault are not uncommon in India; the National Crime Research Bureau reported that only 29 percent of those accused of rape were convicted: publicized instances include the Park Street gang-rape case of 2012, the Delhi gang rape of 2012, the rape of a Mumbai journalist in 2013, the Kamduni gang-rape case of 2014, the rape of an Uber passenger in November 2014, the rape of Asifa in 2018, the Dehradun gang rape in 2018, the Unnao rape victim in 2019, and many more. However, it is the Delhi gang-rape case of 2012 that became sensational and received extended national and international coverage. The brutality associated with the case made it unusual, leading to mass protests and, eventually, to a change in the existing law. Sexual assault coverage in India is male-centric—which is unsurprising, as men control the majority of newsrooms (Hegde, 2011). Media frames and the coverage of sexual assault address patriarchal concerns, such as the perils of a woman working outside the confines of home, issues of safety in urban spaces, and keeping the "honor" of the women and their families, hence the disassociation from feminist activism.

SITUATING THIS RESEARCH AND RESEARCH METHODS

I identify myself as an emerging feminist scholar of media, and, in keeping with the feminist media scholarship on creating alliances within the global system, I have deliberately not focused in this research on analyzing the scholarly gaps on rape scripts based on the Anglo-Western norms of knowledge production. The development of the method of my research is inspired by Lynes's (2012) rationalization of creating alliances within the global system:

> As feminist scholars of global media, we are driven to identify the considerable gaps in our knowledge and practices at the scale of the global, the transnational, or the cross-cultural. This very scale demands an imaginative leap across specific instances in the interest of a critical scholarship that understands and engages the effects of an expansive global capitalism, in the interest of forging sites of solidarity and resistance, and in the service of what Chandra Talpade Mohanty terms a "feminism without borders." Such scales of analysis (in media, activism, and academics) focus on questions of production and reception in cultures of exchange, attending specifically to the differential relationships in the global system and the uneven terms of cooperation, even as the aim of scholarship and cultural production remain to discover possibilities for alliances, alternative histories or new identity positions. (p. 3)

As a third-wave feminist and feminist media scholar, I incorporate the feminist media methods of inclusivity and intersectionality in my research and sample. The emphasis on rape and sexual harassment is the cornerstone of third-wave feminism and it incorporates intersectionality. The feminist methodology is based on a nonhierarchical, interactive approach to feminist research. This methodology influences my selection of a research method that reflects the feminist ideals of equality and interaction (King, 1994). Historically, feminist goals in research also incorporate collaboration, reducing the distance between the researcher and the researched, as well as the emancipation of the researcher (Hesse-Bieber, 2010).

Collaboration has been an important part of this research—instead of the researcher and subject relationship, I have seen my interviewees as collaborators in enlightening me and giving me the opportunity to share their experiences in an academic, theoretical framework, which has contributed greatly to the significance of this project. However, the path of feminist research methods involves taking steps toward erasing hierarchy in the interview process. Instead of the researcher and participant relationship, I have used an informal style of conversation with the feminist activists and journalists. I had a set of questions for the interviewees, but we went with the flow of the conversations, which also gave my interviewees a chance to ask me questions about the research and my framework. This gave me a deeper insight into their views in ways that might not have been possible if I had tried to limit our conversations to my predetermined questions.

Some of their questions were on sexual harassment in the United States and its outcome. Designing a feminist research project is often a reflective process, involving an awareness of privileges and entitlement. I am not hesitant to say that my research for this book helped me to recognize my privileges and disenfranchisement in some situations. One of my aims in writing this book was to bring forth not just the celebratory feminist hashtag activism but also the challenges faced by rural and lower-caste women in their anti-rape feminist activism. I hope that this book helps create a meaningful change in the role of both mass media and social media.

I have looked beyond "data," "data points," and "samples" in my research, instead humanizing them. Feminist research should not be the study of women but for women (Fonow & Cook, 2005)—that is, it should make a case for studying people not to extract knowledge but instead to create beneficial changes. The path of seeking a change has been affective and emotional; I cannot deny that I have wiped away a tear or two when speaking with the activists or even while reading the transcripts. Among a myriad of emotions, I felt guilty about asking some of the participants to relive their ordeals, but I was relieved when some of them said that they felt liberated to speak about the issue and that more people needed to hear about sexual harassment. It was no less than courageous of them to say so; I have never spoken of the many times I have been sexually harassed, beginning at age thirteen. And, of course, I was reliving many of my own personal experiences of sexual harassment and wondering what else I could have done rather than protesting.

I value mixed methods in research for triangulation and verification. In this research, I conducted mixed-methods interviews (qualitative interviews) from 2016 to 2019, thematic analysis of news articles from 2005 to 2018, and social media network analysis. It is important to note here that the internet and the social media network are biased demographically toward those who hold the most power. In the Indian context, this would be individuals who have access to the platforms, who tend to belong to more privileged classes, castes, and locations.

Interviews

I conducted a total of 75 interviews between 2016 and 2019 with thirty-seven feminist activists and thirty-eight journalists. I re-interviewed a few activists and journalists in 2017 and then again in 2018–2019. This helped me in two ways: the first set of interviews was before #MeToo came into the public sphere, and the second set of interviews was after #MeToo and #MeTooIndia became a public conversation. My efforts to recruit a heterogeneous group of activists and journalists were not entirely successful due to challenges and situations beyond my control. Language was a key issue: as I am reasonably fluent in a couple of Indian languages and was reluctant to recruit a translator for the interviews (because I wanted to converse firsthand with the activists and journalists), I limited myself to speaking with activists and journalists who can speak Bengali, Hindi (various dialects), or English. According to the Census report of 2011, Hindi and Bengali are the most spoken languages in India, where 22 languages are recognized as national languages, and over 19,500 languages are spoken ("More Than 19,500 Languages," 2018). I was not able to interview grassroots feminist activists from rural south India because of my inability to speak the various languages of this region. Instead, I relied on urban feminist activists from south India who spoke English.

There were many other challenges along the way. I decided not to include politically affiliated feminist activists in the interview process because, as a former journalist, I found that, in India, they tend to be heavily influenced by the political ideology of their parties, and their actions depend on whether their party is in power. Their actions would be motivated by the party line and not by the true calling of activism. I want to share an interesting anecdote here to substantiate my argument. More than a decade ago, when I was covering the Indian general election in 2009, a national political party aligned to the left had given candidacy to only two women out of forty-two. When I spoke with the leader of the women's wing of the party and asked why only two women had been chosen, she said that it was a decision made by the members of the politburo, and they saw the capabilities of the candidates and not their gender (P. Guha, 2009). The then chairperson of the women's state commission also avoided commenting on how the low number of women would affect women in politics. This is not the only instance, and thus offers evidence that politically affiliated feminist activists align themselves with the political parties, whether or not they support feminist activism. My experience does not exist in a vacuum; this happens over and over again. In 2017, some of the politically aligned feminist activists came down heavily on Raya Sarkar, the young feminist activist who started #MeToo. The politically aligned feminist activists accused the younger feminist activists of encouraging "naming and shaming" perpetrators of sexual harassment, since they publicly and in some cases anonymously shared their experiences of sexual harassment, which had accused some of the feminist allies of being "establishment" feminists (Menon, 2017).

In a strange contradiction, I also faced strict gatekeeping by some of the urban professionalized nongovernmental organizations (NGOs), thwarting my efforts to interview them or other activists affiliated with the organization. As much as feminism is based on the concept of equality of genders and individuals, the core values of feminism were not present in the strict hierarchical organizational structure of these NGOs (nonprofit organizations) in India. For the feminist activists, I decided to email prospective candidates, inviting them to participate.

The co-fielding practice, as identified by Holmgren (2011), a feminist scholar, has been applicable in this research time and again. Journalists and feminist activists would often say during the interviews, "You know how things work here, you were here." Some journalists would say, "You worked with us; you know how this plays out." Every time I was in such a co-fielding situation, I had to intervene politely and ask for more details: "Yes, of course, but can you elaborate more from your perspective?" I cannot deny that co-fielding in some instances was helpful; instead of being an observer, I was considered "an insider." Since I also wanted participants to feel that they were collaborators in this study, I invited them to read the interview transcripts at the end of the interview. Only two feminist activists accepted this invitation. I was surprised and fascinated to find that the rural and subaltern activists had no expectation of receiving anything in return. They truly wanted to share their experiences with me. The co-fielding practices were useful when we were conversing in their preferred language. In fact, that was one of the reasons I decided not to interview any activist or journalist for whom I would have had to hire an interpreter.

Recruitment

Recruiting the participants for this study was a process with many layers. My former journalist colleagues helped me in sharing the information that I wanted to speak with other journalists and activists. Because I went through the journalists, the rural feminist activists were more than willing to indulge me and speak with me about activism. I sent a few cold emails to some of the urban activists and journalists I wanted to interview. A couple of them graciously responded and agreed to speak with me, and some I never heard from. Just a couple asked me where the interview would be published and if I could travel 6,000 miles for the interview. Between 2016 and 2019, I tried time and again to include male feminist activists, but I never got a response to my repeated phone calls, emails, and direct messages through Twitter.

Choosing the "Rapes" for Analysis

I have always struggled to understand why some rapes make the news and lead to policy changes, while others are relegated to the background. An estimated 99 percent of rapes and sexual harassment incidents go unreported in India (Changoiwala, 2019). The reasons for rapes going unreported include the apathy of the police, policy makers, and family members with respect to taking a case forward. To understand which rapes make headlines and sustain public and political conversations and which fall into the gap between activism and the news reports, I decided to choose coverage of rapes resulting in death from 2005, 2012, 2016, and 2018. I did not include rapes and murders of children for the following reasons:

- The policies and laws around child rape and murder are different from adult rape laws.
- As the mother of a child, I could not see myself continuing to interview activists who work on issues related to child rape, sexual abuse, and murder; it would have been overwhelming for me.

I included the Unnao rape at a later stage of the project (in 2019) because I wanted to assess whether candlelight marches, #MeToo, and #MeTooIndia had any impact on rural rapes involving a political leader.

Ethical Challenges

I first encountered ethical challenges and dilemmas during my time at my previous institution when I started gathering data in 2016, some of which I have discussed in other publications. I also encountered several distinct legal and research dilemmas during this project. For example, the Indian legal system prohibits the media, or any publication, from identifying or naming the victims of rape or sexual assault even remotely to avoid any parallel trials by the media in a matter under trial (PTI, 2018); many people, including me, argue that it contributes to the further stigmatization of the women involved. However, coverage of rape and sexual assault is inconsistent; the news media sometimes identify victims, and other times they use aliases. I have discussed this with journalists, feminist activists, and even lawyer friends, none of whom had a plausible explanation.

I also grappled with the question of whether I should refer to the women who had endured rape and sexual violence as "victims" or "survivors" and discussed this dilemma with journalists and feminist activists during interviews. The majority of participants maintained that regardless of the term used (victim or survivor), the plight of the women remains the same. Some of the participants said that the term "survivor" gave the women a sense of empowerment. Yet others said that the use of the term "survivors" instead of "victims" was nothing more than a media stunt. I decided to use the terminology employed in the writings of women who have been raped and have shared—and therefore relived—their experiences with me. In return, as a gesture of solidarity with those who have been sexually assaulted, I refer to the women as victims.

I was also concerned that I was exploiting my feminist research participants by asking them to relive their experiences, so as appreciation, I tried to help them identify a few funding opportunities, which is an ethical concern in this study.

I also struggled with ethical concerns while gathering data from social media platforms. I gathered nonidentifiable data from publicly open and accessible pages on Facebook. Yet, anonymity and confidentiality continue to be issues when data are collected through online platforms. After I completed the data collection using NetViz, an application native to Facebook, it was abruptly discontinued after the investigation of Facebook over disinformation. Ensuring the anonymity of participants in online data collection is difficult, especially since anonymous data from social media platforms can be made identifiable when it is paired with other information (Vitak, Shilton, & Ashktorab, 2016). Online research subjects are sometimes unaware that they are being monitored and are often unable to control the kind of data that are collected for research. Online data subjects also have uneven opportunities to protect their data. Transparency is another challenge for social computing researchers. The various data collection tools such as GitHub, Facebook API, and others simplify the process of collecting data, but researchers must decide whether and how to inform subjects of their presence and methods (AoIR, 2016; Vitak et al., 2016). Further, I acknowledge that any dangers or problems are outweighed by the benefit of doing the research.

As demographic variables such as race, gender, age, socioeconomic status, and level of technical experience influence the selection and usage of social network sites and online forums, data obtained from social media sites can lack representativeness (Vitak et al., 2016).

One of the biggest dilemmas was collecting data from Facebook, as there are no clear guidelines on the collection of publicly available data. For instance, can information from public Facebook groups and/or pages be used for public research? Since I explicated data (comments) from the Facebook pages of the feminist activist groups, I decided to follow the protocols established by multiple institutions such as the Association of Internet Researchers (AoIR) and the Institutional Review Board at my previous institution. Early academic writings on internet privacy espoused a simple standard in which information communicated in a space open to the public could be considered public, whereas information exchanged strictly between two individuals should be considered private and subject to academic protocols related to the acquisition of informed consent per Institutional Review Board guidelines. This definition is still consistently used in academic research, according to which data from an open space are considered publicly available data. Research groups such as the AoIR conform to similar views on gathering data from social media platforms. However, there are still valid concerns as to how researchers should handle "public" data. In the recent past, publicly available data from social media platforms have been used to the detriment of the user or users (Carson, 2014). For instance, did the user intend to make public the data that are publicly available, or is it public because of the accessibility of the platform? The issues of privacy, accessibility, and digital rights of the users are complicated, and they become fraught in the context of limited digital literacy. As material posted by individuals on social media platforms increasingly becomes nonprivate for reasons that are unclear and constantly changing, user intentionality is called into question. On a similar note, Vitak et al. (2016) argue that online research subjects are not always aware of online monitoring and have unequal opportunities to protect their data. On the increasing loss of transparency in online data collection, Vitak et al. argue that while individuals increasingly use privacy settings provided by social networks, researchers allied with the host platforms may still have access to private data. Transparency is another challenge for social computing researchers. While social media's affordances simplify the process of collecting data, researchers must decide whether and how to inform subjects of their presence, methods, and data collection. This also refers to comments and status messages (data) collected from the Facebook pages of the feminist advocacy groups.

Keeping this dilemma in mind, I decided not to identify users who commented on the feminist group pages on Facebook and only referred to open Facebook pages, which are publicly available data. When I re-collected Facebook data in 2018 after #MeTooIndia and #MeToo, I decided not to look for comments but to analyze only the engagement of content through sharing and likes to protect user privacy. I also followed the ethical principles of social media data collection suggested by Vitak et al. (2016) and AoIR (2016):

1. Being transparent about data collection.
2. Ethical deliberation with peers: Discussing the issues with scholars and researchers outside the individuals directly involved, like advisers and committee members.
3. Caution in sharing results.

THE HETEROGENEOUS FEMINIST MOVEMENT IN INDIA

The Indian feminist movement is both ideologically and structurally heterogeneous. According to Roy (2015), the contemporary Indian feminist movement comprises urban and rural organizations, and national, international, and transnational academics and activists from different socioeconomic strata, although the leadership of the Indian feminist movement largely rests with women belonging to the upper and upper-middle classes.

Moreover, feminist activists engage with women's issues across the broad spectrum of identities based on class, language, religion, ethnicity, and caste that define Indian politics and society (Roy, 2015). On this heterogeneity of feminist activism in India, Katzenstein (1989) writes, "The feminist movement in India tends to be multi-associational, ideologically diverse, regionally broad, and concerned with a vast array of issues" (p. 55) and further argues that the diversity of the feminist movement spans the spectrum from reformists to radicals and is concerned with a broad range of issues, including economic hardship, caste, religion, sexual violence, and violence against women. In the recent past, there has been increasing scholarly interest in religious feminism in India, including Hindu feminism and Islamic feminism (Bedi, 2006; Vatuk, 2008).

Kumar (1993) and Katzenstein (1989) identify six types of feminist activist groups in India:

1. *Women's organizations affiliated with political parties.* For example, the All-India Women's Conference is associated with the Congress Party, and the Mahila Dakshata Samiti was created as the women's wing of the Janata Party in 1978; both are governed by the beliefs of the political parties with which they are connected.

2. *Autonomous women's groups.* Autonomous women's groups started in the 1970s, in an effort to distinguish themselves from politically affiliated women's groups. Many women organized themselves into autonomous groups focusing on issues of violence against women, equal pay, and creating other opportunities for women.

3. *Grassroots organizations.* Women at the grassroots level have also played an essential part in the feminist movement. Some examples of grassroots organizations are the Chipko movement (in which people would hug trees to save them from being cut down) and the Shramik Sanghatana movement (the labor movement), through which tribal women protested against harassment, domestic violence, and alcohol consumption by men.

4. *Women's research institutes.* Since the 1970s, many academics and policy institutes studying issues related to women have been advocating for women's rights. These include the Centre for Women's Development Studies in New Delhi; the Institute of Social Studies Trust; the Indian Social Institute Program

for Women's Development in Bombay; and the Research Center for Women's Studies, which is associated with the Shreemati Nathibai Damodar Thackersey Women's University in Bombay.

5. *Women's development organizations.* There has been a rise in the number of feminist NGOs since the 1970s. These are mostly public organizations that work on various issues related to women in urban areas. However, as Roy (2015) and Katzenstein (1989) point out, women's development organizations are controversial. Roy (2015) notes, "NGOs constitute controversial actors within the feminist political field, especially as they become, on the one hand, key players and, on the other, less representative of a specific kind of feminist politics in becoming more transnationalized and professionalized." This culture of professionalized hierarchy and discrimination against grassroots workers has been recorded in various publications such as *Sangtin Yatra (Playing with Fire: Feminist Thought and Activism through Seven Lives in India)*, written by the Sangtin writers (NGO workers in India) and Richa Nagar. In *Sangtin Yatra*, the grassroots workers narrate the discrimination meted out to them by the NGOs during their work as volunteers and activists.

6. *Numerous "old" and "new" voluntary organizations.* These are the religious, caste, ethnic, and nonsectarian organizations that offer voluntary services to low-income women, such as training for employment, legal aid, and health clinics. There are also projects aimed at middle-class women, such as raising funds to build a hostel for working women in urban areas.

Since 2000, there has been increasing emphasis on the rights of the lesbian, gay, bisexual, transgender, and queer community (along with a continued focus on rape and sexual harassment of women). Compared with the older women's organizations, which had an elitist and classist bias and were inclined to operate within the existing social order, the newer feminist activists and organizations have tended to embrace the struggles of all women irrespective of sexuality, class, caste, or religion (Patel & Khajuria, 2016). The Indian feminist movement has also been accused of being casteist and following "Savarna" feminism (caste privileges), which is largely dominated by the upper-caste and upper-class Hindu women (Kappal, 2017). After the #MeToo movement, many anti-caste Dalit activists, such as Christina Dhanaraj (2018), are speaking against the bias within sexual harassment feminist activism in India and the selective outrage over rape and sexual harassment.

FRAMING OF RAPE IN THE NEWS MEDIA

The politics of the newsroom is an essential indication of how rape coverage is constructed in the news. Joseph (2008) indicates that the ethical values followed in Indian newsrooms and the commodification of news ("what sells as news") influence the news discourses on rape. The concept of newsworthiness is employed by journalism scholars to understand the framing of news on rape. Following a similar premise, Hollander and Rodgers (2014) state that the news value of any conflict helps in establishing the stories and the victims as 'worthy.' This classification of worthy and unworthy victims leads to the disparity of coverage between the violent attacks on the women and the perpetrator. Women from marginalized societies are often deemed unworthy of being given that space. The framing of victims as worthy and unworthy leads to the disparity of coverage between the violent attacks on the women and the perpetrator. For example, Christina Dhanaraj writes in 2018 in the context of anti-rape and sexual harassment coverage and protest of Dalit women, "We have not had a single protest matching the scale of what we witnessed for Nirbhaya."[2]

According to Durham (2013), institutional and social media structures of power marginalize women within the media, including the different ways they are framed. The misogynist biases in the content of news coverage of violence against women are not deliberate, but they are a result of a hegemonic ideology perpetuated by elite white men (Gallagher, 2007). These patterns reflect the "common sense" of a society in which women's standpoints are subordinated and news values reflect a dominant ideology invested in the interests of men. Durham (2013, 2015) and Joseph (2008) posit that journalists are unaware of these pre-existing biases, as they operate within a broader social and political context that shapes the reporting on violence against women. Reinforcing this claim, Gallagher (2007) writes that "media content still reflects a masculine vision of the world and what is important" (p. 7). Scholarly studies focus on the need to improve media discourse on rape and sexual abuse. Mendoza (2014), in her report for PRI, writes: "However, while more sexual violence reports seem to make the news lately, much of the coverage still falls short of explaining why and how such attacks happen as well as how they can be prevented, Mejia said. Reports tend to concentrate on the criminal facts of a case, such as suspects, arrests, and trials, she said. News stories also often use language that avoids placing responsibility on perpetrators while seeming to imply the victim's consent."

This succinctly describes the need to change the discourse and the conversation around reporting on rape and sexual assault. In analyzing content on issues of violence against women, the consideration of societal biases and newsroom politics becomes an important external factor. This is particularly relevant in this book since gender, religion, class, and caste biases influence the selection and framing of rape coverage in Indian newsrooms (Joseph, 2008, 2014).

News narratives related to rape and sexual assault tilt toward the virgin-whore dichotomy, constructing victimization and deviancy in media frames, and victim blaming. Frames on rape myths include "women want to be raped," "women deserve to be raped," "women provoke rape," "women need to be raped," and "women enjoy being raped" (Ardovini-Brooker & Caringella-Macdonald, 2002, p. 3).

Other frames focus on the vulnerability of women, consent of the victim, false stereotypes, and misapplying the terms and frames of "deserving to be raped" and "wanting to be raped" (Mendoza, 2014).

Evidence from multiple scholarly articles shows that these rape myths are universal, as similar frame narratives operate globally. In large part, these frames are created because news coverage is based on the dominant perception of race and gender, apart from other factors such as pornography and sexualization in the media. Rape myth frames become relevant in the context of race and gender because news frames constructed on rape myths reinforce misconceptions about race and gender. Rapes of women of color are underreported and ignored by the media, leading to an increase in ignorance, stigma, and myths around rape and sexual assault (DeCapua, 2013). Minority women are devalued through the relative invisibility or minimization of their experiences of rape victimization (Ardovini-Brooker & Caringella-Macdonald, 2002; Dhanraj, 2018).

This deficit in the reporting of incidents of sexual violence is prevalent in most parts of the world (Alat, 2006; Bonnes, 2013; Hegde, 2011; Hollander & Rodgers, 2014). Hollander and Rodgers (2014) chronicle the good victim and the unworthy victim in U.S. media coverage of rape and sexual assault incidents. Bonnes (2013) provides a similar depiction of South African media coverage; Hegde (2011) and Rao (2014) do the same in the context of Indian media coverage, as does Alat (2006) in the context of Turkish media.

The most prevalent form of reporting news of rape involves the "whore" and "virgin" dichotomy (Hollander & Rodgers, 2014). The assaulted woman is a powerless object who has been "violated." The media either sympathize with the virgin victim or chastise the whore who asked for it (Cole & Daniel, 2005; Durham, 2015; Hollander & Rodgers, 2014). To amend this situation, Worthington (2008) proposes that rape news coverage should focus on the victim's perspective in order to minimize the opportunities for audiences to engage in victim blaming and suspect mitigation. Other rape myths, including lack of adherence to feminine norms and rape as retaliation, develop when sexual assault does not conform to the norms of the existing framework of gender roles (Alat, 2006; Franiuk, Seefelt, Cepress, & Vandello, 2008). This victim-blaming position draws its argument from the pillars of patriarchy. By emphasizing the so-called immorality of the victims, their lack of adherence to gender norms, and their careless or provocative behavior, and even by accusing them of inventing the crime, press reports appear oriented toward forgiving the perpetrators. Alat (2006), in her study of Turkish media coverage of victims of rape and sexual assault, focuses on language that is sympathetic toward the perpetrator: "The responsibility of the attacker is reduced by making him invisible. Using passive clauses, the attacker appears unknown or as a stranger, even though later in the text, it is reported that he is an ex-boyfriend or ex-husband. This way of reporting—hiding the attacker's identity—undermines the seriousness of male violence in the society and maintains the myth that the family is a sacred and safe place for women, although the reality might be the opposite" (p. 302).

The hypocritical rape myths in the news coverage—where the popular narrative is that men are the victims of their passion and obsession with women, and women lack moral and social character—indicate the existence of patriarchy in newsrooms (O'Hara, 2012; Worthington, 2008). O'Hara (2012) further focuses on various rape myths in the media, such as the sexualization of victims, by focusing on their dress, makeup, and body. Myths surrounding the perpetrator include being sex-starved or insane. Past and present research indicates that rape myths have damaging outcomes (Ardovini-Brooker & Caringella-Macdonald, 2002; O'Hara, 2012) through stigmatizing women who have been raped or sexually assaulted.

Recent research on myths and frames surrounding rape coverage has reinforced the previous research on frames. DiBennardo's (2018) research on the ideal victim and monstrous perpetrators in rape coverage framing focuses on the representation of rape victims and rapists in the media when the discourse focuses on particular personality traits, portraying them as deviants in society in news media coverage of rape, sexual harassment, and anti-rape activism in India.

The state of the media in any country—its coverage patterns of political, social, and economic issues—tends to reflect the country's internal political situation and culture. India is one of the few countries that, in the recent past, have registered an increase in the circulation of newspapers (Audit Bureau of Circulation, 2017). Seventy percent of the most widely circulated English-language newspapers in India are based in urban India, but 88 percent of the rapes happen in rural India and receive no or only negligible coverage in English-language newspapers (Shah, 2018). Hence, one of the factors leading to the news and social media outrage of the infamous 2012 Delhi gang rape of Jyoti Singh was its location (P. Guha, 2017).

After the 2012 Delhi gang rape of Jyoti Singh, communications and legal scholars began focusing on rape coverage in the Indian news media. The focus of the media framing in the 2012 Delhi gang-rape case was primarily on the protests and the incident (Jolly, 2016; Phillips et al., 2015). Jolly (2016) found that there was almost no victim blaming of Jyoti Singh in the media coverage. Phillips et al. (2015) asserted that there were some instances of victim blaming by controversial spiritual and political leaders, which were reported by the media. These comments criticized the woman for being guilty of being present in a public space at night and wearing a Western-style dress.

I. Nagar (2016) analyzed the news media coverage of Jyoti Singh's gang rape in the two most circulated English and Hindi newspapers in India—namely, the *Times of India* and *Dainik Jagran*—and found that there was a steady increase in the coverage of the incident as the protests peaked. She argues that there was a consistent focus on the middle-class background of the victim, leading to her deification. Jolly (2016) and I. Nagar (2016) agreed that the increased and consistent coverage of Jyoti Singh's rape and murder was an outlier in the Indian media. Unfortunately, there has been no decrease in the incidence of rape and sexual assault in India, nor have the media or scholars taken the issue forward concerning other rape or sexual assault cases. The clock seems to have stopped in 2012 for discussions regarding the framing and news coverage of rape and sexual assault victims. Most scholarly work on rape and sexual harassment coverage in India focuses on Jyoti Singh's rape in 2012. In the interviews I conducted with activists and journalists from 2016 until 2019, analysis of rape coverage from 2005 until 2016, and analysis of the #MeToo movement from 2017 to 2018 it was pointed out that there have been selective changes in rape and sexual harassment coverage, but, mostly, the coverage is still inconsistent.

In 2005, the rape of a call center executive was widely covered by the news media in India. Hegde (2011) discusses the relationship between media coverage and the incidence of sexual assault in India. She writes that the coverage was male-centric—which is unsurprising, as men control the majority of newsrooms—but does not discuss what the media failed to address in this coverage. Media frames and the coverage of sexual assault address patriarchal concerns, such as the perils of a woman working outside the confines of home, issues of safety in urban spaces, and keeping the "honor" of the women and their families. I would venture that the print media refrained from addressing the concerns and expectations of women as individuals rather than as part of a patriarchal family structure.

The discussion of rape myths is tied to societal perceptions. Worthington (2008) explains that "some viewers mobilize progressive elements in the text to reassert assault survivors' perspectives and some draw on resources beyond the text to discuss the rape scandal in patriarchal terms that presume women's responsibility for preventing assault" (p. 346). To maintain objectivity and balance, the press provides equal prominence and coverage to the perpetrators' voices, eventually relegating the victims' stories to lesser importance (Meyers, 1997). Ironically, rape gets more media attention than do other women's issues, although the majority of the time, this attention is superficial and the media focus is on the events rather than the process or the subtext that leads to the incidents of rape and sexual assault (Hegde, 2011).

Women journalists of the Global South have frequently accused Western women journalists of generalizing issues of rape and sexual assault. *Ms.* magazine has tried to resolve this issue by hiring feminist reporters from specifically non-Western countries. One can see here the limitations of merely increasing the number of female journalists in the newsroom without fundamentally challenging the way news works and the inherent cultural bias:

News is typically produced by a western news organization, from a western perspective, and for global consumption. Reporters and sources are western, and women are "othered" through the "neo-traditional" story stance. This lack of context is especially evident in western coverage of crimes against women in the Global South. While little attention to women's issues in the news media might be seen as a step forward, the debate about a potential global, homogenizing feminism shows that certain well-intended representations might be problematic. One of the main concerns is that women in "other" cultures are represented as victims without an understanding of their varied local context. (Geertsema, 2009, p. 17)

Violence against women can be best understood when it is explained using the intersectional identity lens. Gangoli (2011) looks at rape and sexual assault together with the intersectional identity of the woman. What is her position in society? Is she highly educated? Is she from the city or a rural area? What is her economic position? Is "her story" valuable for the media and policy makers? The "status" of the woman within the family and outside the family is significant in the context of the focus that it receives from the media, law enforcement, the public, and policy makers.

Past research on activism and internet platforms argues that access to the internet and various digital platforms enables grassroots activists to penetrate the elite hold on the media, where the advocacy groups first create a campaign for online platforms and then replicate the same campaign for other media platforms (Chadwick, 2013; Chadwick & Smith, 2016). But this media system is essentially based on First World countries, which have relatively high internet penetration rates and low digital divides. In a digitally emerging country like India, for any activist group or movement to build a public and political agenda on a contentious issue such as rape and sexual harassment, advocates need to work simultaneously with social media, news media, and journalists (P. Guha, 2015). In a digitally emerging country like India, the relationship between social media platforms and mainstream media in feminist activism should be more simultaneous, interdependent, and concurrent to build an agenda, while a campaign on an issue should be focused equally on digital platforms and on the news media. In India, for example, this dependence of grassroots activists on the internet is often reversed. The grassroots activists rely on journalists and the mainstream news media to get and disseminate information.

Ianelli (2016), in her book *Hybrid Politics: Media and Participation*, similarly proposes moving "beyond the single medium approach" in activism and political participation (p. 36) and instead focusing on the co-existence of diverse forms of media to promote social and political participation.

Universally, rape and sexual assault media coverage share certain similarities, such as doubting the claims of the victim or survivor and, to a large extent, shaming them. Women of marginalized communities have to face further indignities due to their social and economic position. Their stories are lost in the daily news cycle and in the social media outrage over "prominent" rapes and sexual harassment. However, every country and culture has a varied set of economic, social, and political frameworks, which are the deciding factor for how media and the internet operate in the country. What works in some countries may not work in others, and that holds true for digital activism against rape and sexual harassment as well. In any digitally emerging country, therefore, it is important to focus on all forms of media to build a public agenda against rape and sexual assault.

THE NEWS INDUSTRY IN INDIA

The news media industry in India has been a pillar of the fourth estate since the pre-independence period. The newspapers, both English- and Indian-language papers, played an important role during the independence movement and in the post-independence period in both policy making and nation building. In 1977, the Indian press witnessed and experienced one of its most difficult situations during the censorship of the press. Since the 1990s, however, the Indian press has seen a tremendous shift in its content and presentation owing to the liberalization of the economy.

The Indian news media initially emerged in the eighteenth century under British colonial rule (Otis, 2019; Thomas, 2006). The British colonizers set up the first English-language press in India, *Hickey's Bengal Gazette*, followed later by other newspapers in English and regional languages established by Indian industrialists and educationists (Rodrigues & Ranganathan, 2015). The leading English newspapers during pre- and post-independent India were the *Times of India*, the *Hindustan Times*, and *The Hindu* (Statista, 2019). The Indian press was a pillar of support for the Indian independence movement. After independence, the Indian news media industry has exercised relative freedom compared with its neighbors, such as Pakistan and Myanmar (Rana, 2014). Even now, according to Freedom House, India consistently ranks higher in media freedom compared with its immediate neighbors. However, it would be wrong to say that the history of the Indian media has been without blemish. During the Indian emergency of 1975, declared by the then prime minister Indira Gandhi, there was unprecedented censorship of the press for two years (Rodrigues & Ranganathan, 2015; Tarlo, 2001).

The Indian news media industry has seen tremendous growth since the economic reforms of 1991, leading to increased privatization of organizations, new communications technology, and the establishment of India's position as a global market and economy (Bhargavi, Guru, and Joseph, 2015; Rodrigues & Ranganathan, 2015). India constitutes the largest market for newspapers in the world, followed by China and Japan (Bhargavi, Guru, & Joseph, 2015). The growth of Indian regional news media revolutionized the Indian print news industry by increasing revenue and circulation (Jeffrey, 2000). According to the annual report published in March 2018 by the Registrar of Newspapers in India, there are 118,239 registered publications in India, including 17,573 daily newspapers. According to another report published in March 2016 by the Ministry of Information and Broadcast, India, there are 403 television news channels in India. Both reports indicate that the mainstream news media in India have been steadily growing at a time when the news media in the rest of the world are declining (Kilman, 2015a).

In the first quarter data of 2019 of the Indian Readership Survey, indicated that newspaper readership in India has grown from 407 million to 425 million between 2017 to 2019. The report was released by the Media Research Users Council (MRUC) on Friday: "While Hindi and regional dailies grew at 3.9 percent and 5.7 percent, respectively, English newspapers saw a 10.7 percent growth, though on a small base. Hindi dailies had 186 million readers, while regional readership stood at 211 million in IRS Q1 2019. English newspaper readership went up from 28 million to 31 million between the 2017 and Q1 2019 surveys" (Malvania, 2019).

According to the Audit Bureau of Circulations in India, newspaper sales in the country increased by 15 percent in 2014 (cited in Bhargavi et al., 2015). However, advertising in print news media has declined due to an increase in broadcast media and internet-based services (Manjappa, 2014). To attract younger readers, the Indian print media business heavily subsidizes digital journalism (Manjappa, 2014). As has been documented in other parts of the world, the newspaper industry is gradually dying, with many titles going out of print and some laying off newsroom staff (Mitchell & Holcomb, 2016). According to the State of the Media Report 2016, published by the Pew Research Center, newsrooms are undergoing budget cuts and layoffs; in 2014, employment in print newsrooms declined by 10 percent, and circulation fell by 1.3 percent in North America (Kilman, 2015b). However, circulation rose by 9.8 percent in Asia in 2014 from a year earlier, by 1.2 percent in the Middle East and Africa, and by 0.6 percent in Latin America (Kilman, 2015a). The newspaper business in India is still the strongest print newspaper industry in the world (Bhargavi et al., 2015; Kilman, 2015a). This evolution of an expanded media market has also had its share of pitfalls. Manjappa (2014), in his research on the Indian media industry, notes: "The Press Council of India has taken serious note of certain unhealthy practices of Indian press such as concentration of ownership, devaluation of editorial functions, hyper- commercialization, price wars, paid news, private treaties with corporate, bribe-taking, and downgrading the professional ethics and social obligations. The champions of social responsibility of press have called upon the press to function responsibly in India under the changed circumstances."

Ammu Joseph, in an interview in 2019 on the #MeToo movement and the Indian news media, discussed the deeply flawed redressal system in the Indian media organization and its inability to sustain the movement (Mishra, Swaminathan, & Jayakumar, 2019).

The continued growth and popularity of the print news industry and its proven ability to create a public and political agenda (Ram, 2016) supported my decision to focus on the Indian print news media for this study. At the same time, it is important to note that the Indian news media are different from their Western counterparts; in India, the news media are privately owned and operated, and the owners are affiliated with political parties.

2 · FRAMING OF RAPE IN THE NEWS MEDIA AND ITS IMPACT ON FEMINIST ACTIVISM AND JOURNALISTS

#MeTooIndia Including Themes

When I started my research in 2016 after conducting interviews with Indian feminists and journalists over the course of six months, I found that rural-based feminists and journalists and younger fourth-wave online feminists were more forthcoming than were established urban activists. In the process of writing this book and having multiple conversations in the wake of #MeToo in 2018, not much has changed.

In October 2017, Raya Sarkar, a feminist activist, initiated a crowdsourced list of Indian academics involved in sexual harassment of students in higher education. I recognized some of the names. During my time in college, my fellow students and I had a whisper campaign to let our junior cohorts know which professors to avoid during office hours, as we were informed the same way by our senior cohort. However, Raya's list—known as #LoSHA (list of sexual harassers in academia)—received a backlash from the established feminists, who joined forces to support some of the names and called the list a witch hunt because there was no due process.

In 2018, #MeToo focused on celebrities, journalists, and media organizations and released the names of sexual harassers in these professions. There is now also a #MeTooIndia campaign, erasing #LoSHA and Raya Sarkar's work in digital feminism. Surprisingly, there has not been any conversation about the experiences of the semi-urban, rural, lower-caste, or lower-class journalists or entertainment industry workers in #MeToo in 2018. The #MeTooIndia campaign became popular within the context of the urban Indian population, overlooking and neglecting the experiences of women journalists working in Indian-language and rural publications.

What started as a Twitter hashtag conversation quickly spread to other platforms such as Facebook, where victims and survivors shared their experiences as Facebook statuses and sent direct messages to each other. However, the experiences were not shared and known to the majority of the country until they were covered by the mainstream news media. It was not surprising to see that the mainstream news media were standoffish when their editors and journalists were accused. A flag bearer and watchdog against rape and sexual harassment, some of these news media organizations have actively participated in building an anti-rape and sexual harassment public and political agenda (e.g., during the #Nirbhaya campaign after the rape and murder of Jyoti Singh, also infamously known as the Delhi gang rape of 2012).

Unfortunately, since 2012 there have been many rapes, sexual assaults, and sexual harassment incidents in India, but they have not had the same impact as in 2012. This may be because rape or sexual assault is a political rather than a social issue. The end of 2012 and early 2013 were important years in Indian politics because the general elections happened in 2014; similarly, 2019 was an election year, but rape and sexual assault did not feature prominently as a campaign issue. Sexual harassment and rape have become political issues and receive more attention from the media.

However, as I pointed out earlier, such conversations are not inclusive; there have been national and international headlines in the media, but the voices of rural, semi-urban, and Indian local language journalists are still missing and largely muted on social media platforms. A couple of newspapers and news websites published the experiences of local language journalists and rural journalists, but they did not become the focus of the nation's attention, nor did they become part of the hashtag conversations. In all likelihood, their experiences were shared because of a lack of a network. They are fighting their own battles because of the seeming apathy and echo chambers of hashtags.

I interviewed some activists and journalists again in 2018, asking them a similar question about how they helped in anti-rape and sexual harassment agenda building in India, but the context was different in 2018 following the #MeToo and #MeTooIndia era. Even in the #MeToo and #MeTooIndia era, the rural and urban feminist activists and journalists experienced and saw the impact of the movement differently.

ANTI-RAPE AND SEXUAL HARASSMENT AGENDA BUILDING

Journalists participate in creating an agenda for the audience, as a case study by Iyengar demonstrated in 1970. The building of an agenda by journalists has been a constant since time immemorial, irrespective of the media platform or country. However, the agenda-building capacity of the media has been changing and shifting due to the social media platforms and their disruption of gatekeeping by the mainstream media. Many scholars have recently claimed that the increase in the agenda-building capacity of the social media platforms has forced the mainstream media platforms to change their functioning and agenda-setting capacity. However, this is relevant and true in the context of digital First World countries, where the primary audience has shifted to social media platforms for gathering news. The digital divide and digital literacy are still pertinent issues in some regions, which prevents control over the agenda by social media platforms alone. Similarly, in the context of India, #MeTooIndia reflects the setting of the agenda by a select few on social media platforms catering to the urban population. Initially, the mainstream media had a muted response because survivors had accused many of the newsrooms of turning a blind eye to the problem. In response to the pressure from social media citizens, and to save their brand, they have churned out many editorials and articles focused on their position.

Desai (2018), a social commentator and policy maker, has described the #MeToo and #MeTooIndia movements as a continuation of the Nirbhaya movement after Jyoti Singh was brutally gang-raped. Both the #Metoo and #Nirbhaya movements impact urban women in India who identify with the survivors and victims and who also have more access to social media platforms to drive the social movement and work toward a hashtag movement. But the survivors and victims who are in the locational periphery often slip through the cracks because of their limited access to social media platforms, difficulties with identifying with others, and the lack of interest of the journalists and social media crusaders in working with and amplifying the stories of the marginalized survivors and victims. As of December 2018, digital penetration in India is 40 percent, a figure that is possible due to the increasing access in rural areas ("Internet users in India to reach 627 million in 2019," 2019).

Some practitioners and scholars (Singh, 2016; Verma, 2016) attribute this involvement of rural population in anti-rape sexual harassment activism to the intersectional identities of class and caste, and the privilege of having access to technology. However, there has been a negligible focus on location. Location is an important factor in the amplification and agenda-building capacity. Only one newspaper published the experiences of subaltern and local-language women journalists and activists in the #MeToo second wave in India. The #MeToo movement worked when women started using social media platforms to share their experiences with others. But at the same time, a wave focusing on the individual incidents was neglected.

SCRIPTING RAPE AND SEXUAL ASSAULT

Discussion of rape and sexual assault in certain communication practices in some cultures focuses on the "status" of women and the power hierarchy in the society, particularly in the context of India (Bhattacharya, 2017; Gangoli, 2011). Silver (1988), in her discussion of rape, succinctly describes how rape laws are constructed to discredit the woman's perception of the rape: "Whose subjectivity becomes the objectivity of 'what happened' is a matter of social meaning, that is, it has been a matter of sexual politics" (p. 90).

The rape script approach is also intertwined with discussions on access to public spaces and the culture of shaming. Ghosh (2008) suggests that the culture of shaming the woman is instrumental in barring women from public places in India. Bhattacharyya (2014) also notes that the fear of being raped, assaulted, or "violated" forces women to dress traditionally in public spaces and commute by segregated "ladies only" compartments on trains. The responsibility is wholly on women to safeguard their bodies from being violated. Their bodies and their sexuality are encoded as the honor of the family, which can be "violated" (Bhattacharyya, 2014). Women's studies scholars indicate that the "who" in "who has been raped" describes the construction of the rape script. Rao (2014) writes, "Rape is a unique crime, as the society in India inflicts more suffering on the victim than on the perpetrator" (p. 23). The discourse around rape and sexual assault in women's studies has been focused on the social and legal status of women in society.

Gangoli's (2011) work looks at rape and sexual assault in terms of the intersectional identity of the woman. What is her position in society? Did she receive a higher education? Is she from the city or the rural areas? What is her economic position, and is "her story" valuable to the media and the policy makers? The "status" of the woman within the family and outside the family is significant in the context of the focus that it receives from the media, law enforcement, the public, and policy makers.

Krishnan's (2014) work discusses the incidence of rape and/or sexual assault as being a double bind for modern Indian women: on the one hand, the possibility of being raped in public spaces constantly haunts women; on the other hand, the new opportunities encourage them to work outside their homes. Krishnan perceives rape discussion in India as a discourse about the responsibility and self-care of the women.

Feminist Media Theorizing of Mass Media

The #MeToo movement has circled back to the discussion of the feminist theorizing of media and social media platforms. It is imperative to comprehend the theorizing of the social media platforms and the evolving feminist movement by explicating feminism and feminist theories. The history of feminism is embedded in the struggle for equality of women. With the passage of time, the feminist movement transformed its original mandate, resulting in the various waves of the movement. The central focus of feminism is to achieve political, social, economic, and personal equality between genders, irrespective of race, class, or sexuality (Gamble, 2001). Bailey and Chris (2008) provide a moral and ethical framework for the meaning of feminism. According to them, feminism is a response to female oppression, spread over time. It is also based on the claim that men's subordination of women is a fundamental moral wrong. Feminist theories emerged during the feminist movements as a response to understand the feminist discourses in philosophy and different branches of academia (Bailey & Chris, 2008). Each wave of feminism was a response to the previous wave. The first wave of feminism emerged in the late nineteenth and early twentieth centuries against the backdrop of urbanization, industrialization, and liberal and socialist politics. The "wave" formally began at the Seneca Falls Convention in 1848, where Elizabeth Stanton drafted the famous Seneca Falls Declaration proclaiming the goals and ideology of providing opportunities for women, especially including them in political suffrage (Cullen-DuPont, 2009, pp. 234–235). However, the first wave of feminism was limited to the demographic of white, middle-class women. The second wave of feminism came much later, in the 1960s, intertwined with the other movements of the time—the civil rights movement and the anti–Vietnam War movement. Owing to its link with the other social movements, women of color also participated in the feminist movement (Thornham, 2001). The second wave also inculcated the feminist theorization of disciplines, leading to the emergence of the discipline of women's studies in academia. This was a complex and diverse wave, as it propagated the idea that sexism and oppression of women are a consequence of the interconnection of gender, race, and class (Alcoff, 2012). It also made an important distinction between sex and gender, based on biological differences and social construction (Thornham, 2001). The third wave of feminism came in the late 1980s to early 1990s and included issues of gender violence, rape, and reproductive rights (Yu, 2009). I am a self-proclaimed third-wave feminist, with a strong belief that the fourth wave of feminism has also arrived, in which we are experiencing the use of the internet in challenging misogyny and sexism. Some scholars and activists have defined the fourth wave of feminism as being "online" (Schulte, 2011). However, this has been challenged on the grounds that increased usage of the internet is not enough to define a new era. "But it is increasingly clear that the Internet has facilitated the creation of a global community of feminists who use the Internet both for discussion and activism" (Munro, 2013).

In the past, both feminist theorizing in social science disciplines and the feminist movement were limited to the demographic of white women of Western countries. Gradually, transnational feminism in the global context became a platform for international feminists of the Global South. In the present context, feminist media theorization has thrived on transnational feminism. I argue that the origin of feminist theorizing in the media is due to the influence of the second-wave feminist movement in the media industry. In the following excerpt, Cantor (1988) provides a timeline for the activism of second-wave feminists in the mass media industry:

> Feminists paid particular attention to the fairness shown women by the media. Underlying the feminist political agenda of the time, in addition to guaranteeing equality in economic and social roles, was the demand for a cultural change in the ways women were depicted. In addition to how women were portrayed in programs, feminist critics charged media owners and managers with sexism. They supported this claim with reports showing widespread discrimination against women in broadcast industry employment practices. When a man and a woman applied for a job, most often, the man was hired. If hired, the woman was probably paid a salary lower than that the man would have been given. The woman also would have been on a slower promotion track, if any. In terms of portrayal, critics claimed that women were stereotyped and trivialized in programs and advertisements. Not until the 1970s did these critics organize into groups to attempt through legal channels to have more women hired in decision-making positions and to change the ways women were depicted on the screen. Feminist activists working primarily through women's organizations, especially the National Organization for Women (NOW), adopted the methods that other minority groups had used to try to achieve more equal treatment in media presentations and equity in employment. (p. 76)

Theories of mass media and journalism have been based on their effects on the audience and the political system. Diverse feminist theories have been applied to mass media research, and this scholarship is widely known as feminist media theories (Harp, 2008). Feminist theorization of media studies seeks to understand the portrayal of women in popular media and news media, the status of women journalists in newsrooms, and coverage of violence against women in popular media and news media. However, this list is not conclusive; there are other issues studied within the scholarship of feminist media theories. Media studies use an array of theories to study the relationship between media and audience, media and civil society, media and government, and media and politics. Scholars employ diverse lenses to understand these patterns within the discipline of media studies. Feminist theorization of mass media investigates the functions of journalism and media in the context of conventional feminist theories. Harp (2008) discusses this extensively in his study of journalism and the feminist framework through four approaches to feminist media theorization: (1) an approach criticizing stereotypical media representation of women, (2) an approach revealing an alternate portrayal, (3) an ideological approach accounting for the political and economic nature of representation, and (4) a semiotic approach focusing on audience and reception (p. 296). Other recent approaches include the sender–receiver model based on the newer paradigms of feminist approaches to communication, including stereotype and socialization, pornography, and ideology (Van Zoonen, 1994) and agency of women in media production (Ross & Carter, 2011).

Ross and Carter (2011), in their study of newsroom processes and socialization, employ feminist media studies theory. The following is their analogy of feminist media studies based on past research: "Feminist media studies examining the processes of socialization into the newsroom, where reporters learn on a daily basis the skills needed for their job, show that historically, assumptions about gender-appropriateness have actually been central to definitions of the profession (Djerf-Pierre and Lofgren-Nilsson, 2004; Steiner, 1998; Steiner et al., 2004)" (Ross & Carter, 2011, p. 1149).

I posit that the feminist theories of media studies are advantageous to comprehend issues beyond newsroom values and functions. Feminist theorizing in journalism and mass media has usually focused on the representation of women in mass media, gendered newsroom values, and audience reception of stereotypical portrayals (Harp, 2008).

Feminist Theorization in the Media

To discuss feminist theorization in the media further, it is crucial to understand the different facets of feminism in the context of mass media research. According to Steeves (1987), feminist media research is mostly informed by four schools of thought: liberal feminism, Marxist feminism, socialist feminism, and radical feminism. Steeves (2001) adds to her previous essay three more schools of feminism: post-structural feminism, postcolonial feminism, and Black feminism; however, I will focus on the first four schools she discussed. Radical and structuralist feminist communication scholars focus on texts and often ignore important contextual considerations. "These perspectives are differentiated further according to whether they assume a need for change involving biological manipulations and/or political separatism (radical feminism); individual behavior (liberal feminism); social-psychological factors and individual behavior (cognitive/social learning theories and psychoanalytic-influenced gender theories, including the French feminisms), and/or revolutionary sociocultural and economic events that would affect social-psychological conditions and individuals (Marxist and socialist forms of feminism)" (Steeves, 1987, p. 98).

Radical feminism argues that men control women in patriarchal society because they control the reproductive process. Radical feminists do not seek equality in the same system, but they propose alternate communities exclusively for women to nurture their lives and careers (Steeves, 1987). Liberal feminism is known to have had the most influence on Western feminism (Lennon, 2013). It focuses on the creation and reform of legal policies for the promotion of women's opportunities for intellectual growth and professional success (Lennon, 2013). "Early liberals worked for women's suffrage and property ownership. Contemporary liberals fight for issues such as equal pay and employment" (Steeves, 1987). Steeves (1987) brings forth a limitation of feminist media theorization, which alienates women of color: "Liberal feminism, which characterizes most of the U.S. mainstream media research, speaks only to white, heterosexual, middle- and upper-class women and is incapable of addressing most women's concerns" (p. 102). Marxist and socialist feminism are in contention with radical and liberal feminism. The central thesis of Marxist and socialist feminism is based on class struggle. Class struggle is the root cause of patriarchy and oppression of women (Lennon, 2013). In her research on the feminist theorization of media, Steeves (1987) concluded that socialist feminism has the best potential for "a comprehensive framework to address women's devaluation in communication" (p. 99). Steeves (1987, 2001) demonstrates in her arguments that there is no single feminist theorization of media. The feminist theorization of media is distinctive in its diversity. However, Rakow (2012) theorizes feminism in communication as a single unit and defines feminist theory in communication in the following excerpt:

> Feminist theory in communication is developed and used by scholars to understand gender as a communicative process, with the goal of making social changes important to the well-being of women and, ultimately, everyone. Despite a common purpose, feminist scholars differ on many grounds and typically work in subareas across the discipline of communication. Contemporary feminist theory blossomed among scholars interested in women and communication in the United States in the 1980s, with attention devoted to it in programming in academic communication associations and with a new wave of publishing that theorized, rather than assumed, gender differences.

Although Rakow (2012) uses feminist theory as a singular terminology in her definition, she elaborates that feminist media scholarship is based on various categories of feminist epistemology. I agree with this understanding that feminist theorization in the media is not a single unit, based on the past classifications of liberal, Marxist, and radical feminism and more recent categories of transnational and cyberfeminism. In a study of female journalists reporting on the Australian Football League, Lennon (2013) successfully engages liberal, Marxist, and radical feminist theories to theorize feminist media studies. According to Lennon, the radical feminist response to sports coverage by female journalists would be to abolish the sports system, since it devalues female journalists. The liberal feminist response would be to increase the employment of women in sports newsrooms to provide a female perspective. Substantially increasing the employment of female journalists in newsrooms also decreases the biases against them (Hardin & Shain, 2005; Lennon, 2013). There is, however, not much clarity on the Marxist feminist response to this issue. I would argue that because women in the newsroom are traditionally paid less than men in the same position,[1] they are oppressed in the newsroom.

As discussed earlier, feminist theorizing of media is profoundly influenced by liberal feminism and radical feminism. In my understanding, cultural feminism is an offshoot of radical feminism. "Cultural feminists believed that women had a unique set of interests that could not be understood or served well by men. Those interests stress such things as peace, cooperation, non-violent settlement of differences, and altruism" (Beam & Di Cicco, 2010). Beam and Di Cicco (2010) operationalized cultural feminism in theorizing about newsroom values and cultures when women exclusively manage them. However, I found both their study and the cultural feminist theorization of media to be one-dimensional; there were no discussions of women of color, class, or sexuality. Beam and Di Cicco posit that "feminized" newsroom cultures would emphasize feminine topics and de-emphasize masculine topics. However, there is no discussion of how the "feminized" newsroom cultures might be experienced differently by women of color and immigrant women.

Some scholars believe that feminist media theorizing based on radical, Marxist, liberal, and cultural feminism is inadequate (Gallagher, 2007; Van Zoonen, 1994). To include the voices of women of color and women from the Global South in feminist media theorizing, it is essential to introduce the feminist standpoint epistemology, transnational feminism, and the concept of intersectionality.

Feminist standpoint epistemology (FSE) is based on the scholarship of knowledge, truth, and lived experiences of marginalized groups (Hartsock, 2004). Brooks (2007) provides a simplified explanation of FSE: "Feminist standpoint epistemology is a unique philosophy of knowledge building that challenges us to (1) see and understand the world through the eyes and experiences of oppressed women and (2) apply the vision and knowledge of oppressed women to social activism and social change. Feminist standpoint epistemology requires the fusion of knowledge and practice" (p. 55).

Steiner (2013) offers an outstanding theorization of FSE in the study of journalism and ethics. Steiner explains how the principles of FSE can be used in newsrooms to incorporate the experiences of marginalized groups without misconstruing newsroom objectivity. Steiner defines FSE as the following: "Feminist Standpoint Epistemology (FSE) seeks knowledge that is less false, including by being less ethnocentric and less sexist. FSE offers a real-world, practical account of how to understand knowledge as socially situated, a condition that both limits and enables what one can know" (p. 113).

In the instances shared by Steiner in this essay, I can relate to a particular one based on my lived experiences as a woman journalist in my country of nationality and as a woman journalist of color in other countries. Steiner (2013) theorizes that the personal experiences of journalists influence their coverage in a positive way based on their insights. FSE makes this possible; therefore, instead of a conflict of interest, this can be an advantage (p. 129), as FSE makes it possible for women of color and other marginalized groups to cover incidents from their perspectives in journalism. I hypothesize that FSE accommodates minority groups within the purview of feminist theorizing in the media. As I discussed earlier, the initial theories of feminism—radical, liberal, and Marxist—had minimal scope to accommodate minority groups, and FSE works as a catalyst in overcoming this situation.

As a woman of color and an immigrant in a Western country, I am personally invested in the framework of intersectionality and transnational feminism. Mohanty (2003) describes the transnational feminist practice as "building feminist solidarities across the divisions of place, identity, class, work, belief, and so on" (p. 251). Shome (2006) paraphrases Spivak (1999) and Mohanty (2003), the leading scholars of transnational feminism, to describe transnational feminism: "The category 'woman of color' in which so much of critical race and 'multicultural' feminism has invested its energy becomes somewhat meaningless unless we are willing to stretch and situate it across the macro- and micro-cultural, historical, spatial, temporal, and economic relations that connect and disconnect (in unequal ways) the symbolic, emotional, psychic, and material lives of women and men in diverse parts of the world" (p. 256). A simplified version of transnational feminism may be defined as building sisterhood across borders between feminist activists and researchers. It also critiques the hegemonic discourse of Western mainstream feminism for trying to "save" women of color or other nationalities (Mohanty, 2003). In trying to explain the hegemonic discourse in Western media, Narayan (1997) chronicles her frustration when she encounters one-sided phrases such as "women are being burned to death every day in India" (p. 83). According to Narayan, this phrase frames all Indian women as victims of patriarchy, without considering the existing intersections of class, caste, and religion. *Oprah* magazine has also been accused of this framing, in which all girls from the Global South are stereotyped as victims (Geertsema, 2009).

Shome (2006) stimulates the discussion of transnational feminism by providing instances of transnational feminist theorization of the media in the following excerpt:

> Transnational feminist media scholars have thus investigated issues such as how diasporic ethnic groups in the United States utilize media texts (Maira, 2002; Valdivia, 2003) to stage new hybrid visions of "community" . . . how western media texts circulate, are utilized, and interpreted in unpredictable ways by women in non-western cultures in which these texts serve both as sites of pleasure and resistance to traditional norms while also functioning as vehicles through which the West is "othered" and local/national values restored (Parameswaran, 2003b); how

transnational flows of sexually laden texts including those that centralize female desire and erotics are often framed, received, and given meaning through local politics around gender and sexuality (LaPastina, 2004; Moorti, 2000); and how the circulation of iconic images of western women in non-western contexts are utilized to shore up "modern" national (consumerist) subjectivities in which these images become saturated with local inflections (Zacharias, 2003). Taken together, these works illuminate a central theoretical impulse that informs transnational feminist interrogations of "audience." (pp. 264–265)

Ironically, Shome (2006), in this thought-provoking passage, does not discuss the concept of intersectionality. I suggest that intersectionality and transnational feminist theorizing of media are interdependent. The concept of intersectionality denotes the various ways in which race and gender interact. Race, gender, and other identity categories are most often treated as biases in mainstream and dominant academic dialogues (Crenshaw, 1991).

Intersectionality becomes a way to understand the shifting, fluid, and complex natures of all our inherited and social identities. One's race, class, gender, and nationality give us insight into the complexity of intersections. In this context, Crenshaw's study of violence against women of color is groundbreaking. I will engage this theorization of intersectionality to discuss rape myths in media coverage and show that intersectionality is appropriate in the feminist theorization of media. Although Sengupta (2006) critiques Crenshaw's analysis that intersectionality defines individual identities in rigid, tiny boxes, I think Sengupta misinterprets Crenshaw. The intersections that Crenshaw examined are not fixed, and they are not representative of identity as a totality, but each is fluid.

Transnational Feminist Theorization and Digital Activism

Intersectionality is a transformative theory owing to its fluidity, which cannot be separated from activism. Intersectionality is concerned with the lived experiences and struggles of women of color and other marginalized groups. Intersectionality also explores the complexities and shiftability of individual identities of race, class, gender (Yu, 2009; Collins, 1998). The intersection between individual and group identities creates variations within groups, and creates the multifaceted nature of power relations (Yu, 2009). The third-wave feminist movement has been a significant resource for transnational women and their activism. Although some scholarship has been critical of the third wave, accusing it of contextualizing issues from Western perspectives (Yu, 2009), I argue that third-wave feminism provides a platform and context to transnational feminism and intersectionality. For instance, violence against women is a fundamental issue in the third-wave feminist movement. Violence against women can be best understood when it is explained using the transnational feminist paradigm and the intersectional identity lens. Similarly, as I discussed earlier, transnational feminist theorization is becoming manifest in the coverage of rape and sexual assault internationally (Durham, 2015).

Feminist media theorization and women's media activism have been interwoven to emphasize the meaningful participation of women in the media and transform the myths associated with coverage of women (Minic, 2008). Therefore, feminist media theorizing and activism are not divorced from one another. However, feminist media scholars have accused feminist media activists of immersing their theoretical groundwork in liberal or radical feminism (Minic, 2008; Van Zoonen, 1994). This is where I argue that transnational feminist media theorization makes a contribution to digital activism. By definition, transnational feminism encompasses ethnic, national, religious, sexual, and class differences (Thayer, 2001). Transnational feminism is similar to digital activism, where communities are formed to provide a voice and space to marginalized groups. Digital activism refers to the use of digital technology in an activist campaign in the context of political, social, and economic factors that impact on the use of digital infrastructure (Joyce, 2010).

Transnational feminist theorization is crucial to explaining feminist theorization in digital activism. This growing body of scholarship in the area of feminist theorization in digital activism is inclined toward a transnational theory of feminism and intersectionality. When #BlackLivesMatter became a dominant source of activism on the internet, the activism focused on only male victims of police brutality. An alternate feminist hashtag, #SayHerName, was propagated by Black feminist activists in response to the missing coverage and discussion of Black women and women of color who were similarly victims of police brutality. The internet and media represent contested terrains in which alternate subcultural forces are articulated as a response to conservative and hegemonic forces (Kahn & Kellner, 2012). Digital spaces are not just spaces for identity formation but also platforms to express intersectional ideology, cultural hegemony, and politics (Leurs & Ponzanesi, 2014). This can be explained by a case study; when feminist media critic Anita Sarkeesian was targeted in social media networks for her campaign against sexist video games, the digital activism campaign #GamerGate emerged on social media platforms. Sarkeesian engaged in this activism using her intersectional identity as a Canadian American woman of Iraqi Armenian descent. Digital activism has also facilitated the creation of transnational feminist communities, as in the cases of Black Twitter and feminist Twitter. The internet provides a space for marginalized groups to voice their opinions and construct their activism, for "groups and individuals excluded from mainstream politics and cultural production of Internet technopolitics and culture" (Kahn & Kellner, 2012, p. 600). However, Kahn and Kellner also add a note of caution that it would be naive to assume that the internet is just a democratic and participatory platform; it has a robust commercial and economic function.

A discussion of digital activism based on the framework of feminist media theorization would be incomplete without considering cyberfeminism. Cyberfeminism is described as a movement using technology to note and combat inequality in digital, physical, and ideological spaces (Schulte, 2011). Cyberfeminism has facilitated women from diverse spaces to collaborate on activism. For instance, feminist digital activism has usually been assumed to be feminist activism and a radical political movement of white Western women (Khamis, 2010; Yu, 2009). I hypothesize that the collaboration between transnational feminism and cyberfeminism has encouraged intersectional feminist discourses in digital media, leading to digital activism. For instance, Khamis (2010) attributes the rise of Islamic feminism to discourses in cyberfeminism. Islamic feminism may seem to be a contradictory proposition, owing to the dichotomy between the religious restrictions and the struggle to bring about equality of genders (Khamis, 2010). The digital space and activism embolden Muslim women to protest and share knowledge against male hegemony within the Islamic norms and values.

Explicating Rape Myths in the Media

Feminist theorization in the media can be invoked to understand the coverage of rape and sexual assault. The trajectory of scholarship on rape myths and news values is core to the discussion of intersectionality. Discourses on rape and sexual assault in journalism are constructed on the censorship of the media and the framing of the incidents. Journalism scholars note the dichotomy in reporting on sexual assaults—on the one hand, there is censorship of reportage on rape and sexual assault; on the other hand, the limited coverage includes sexualization and victimization of the woman (Joseph, 2008; Rao, 2014). This trend is universal in the context of rape and sexual assault (Durham, 2015; Rao, 2014). Journalism scholars writing on rape also theorize transnational feminism and media representation. Durham (2015) draws heavily on transnational feminism in the context of the Delhi gang rape in December 2012, probing the gendered and sexualized politics of space and time. The politics of what prevails in the newsroom is also an important indication of how rape coverage is constructed in the news. As I have indicated previously, the commodification of news impacts news framing, discourse, and audience engagement on rape and sexual violence issues. In her scholarship, Joseph (2008) identified that commercialization of the media impacts the newsworthiness of rape and sexual violence. Hollander and Rodgers (2014) argue that the "news value of conflict, which helped establish the stories as 'worthy,' was tied to the disparity between the violent attacks on the women and the perpetrator." Their study of news frames and the newsworthiness of rape incidents is based on the hegemony theory. The epicenter of rape discourses in journalism focuses primarily on rape and sexual assault as a result of popular media, and the secondary focus is on the structural issues of societal hierarchy and spatial politics. This framework of the commodification of news value and the associated dominance over the bodies of women can be theorized within the framework of Marxist-socialist feminist theory in the media.

Myths and Dichotomies in Reporting Sexual Violence

The dichotomies involved in reporting on the incidence of sexual violence are universal. To amend this situation, Worthington (2008) proposes that when rape news coverage focuses on the victim's perspective, it helps minimize the opportunities for audiences to engage in victim blaming and suspect mitigation. Victim blaming, adherence to feminine norms, women falsely claiming to have been raped for revenge, and other rape myths also develop when sexual assault does not conform to the norms of the existing framework (Alat, 2006; Franiuk et al., 2008). This victim-blaming position draws its argument from the pillars of patriarchy. By emphasizing the morality of the victims, their adherence to gender norms, and their careless or provocative behavior, and even accusing them of inventing the crime, press reports seem to be oriented toward pardoning the perpetrators. The stories are developed in a paradoxical frame where the narrative that males are only the victims of their passion and their obsession with women is juxtaposed with contentions hinted at in the stories that signal male dominance in society (O'Hara, 2012; Worthington, 2008).

O'Hara (2012) further focuses on the various rape myths in the media, like the sexualization of the victims. Myths surrounding the perpetrators include the ideas that they are sex-starved or insane. The rape framing is usually associated with the perpetrator as the monstrous, heinous man committing the crime on a virginal woman or the promiscuous woman who asked the normal man to rape her! However, physical harm and assault on a woman are reported much later in the report. While some journalists may deliberately employ these myths to sensationalize a story (O'Hara, 2012), the onus of responsibility to establish rape accusations is always on the victims of sexual assault. Determining whether rapes are real depends on factors like victim blaming, defending rapists, and claims about the incidence of false rape reports. Past and present studies of rape myths indicate the damaging outcomes of rape myths. Ardovini-Brooker and Caringella-Macdonald (2002) refer to past research on the accountability of the news media in reinforcing societal perceptions: "News coverage buttresses dominant preconceptions, or rather, misconceptions, about women, men, and sexual violence. Rape is the only crime in which the victim's actions are judged to demonstrate the lack of consent (Carlen, 1994; MacKinnon, 1993, 1987, cited by Madriz, 1997, p. 19). Imagine a victim of a carjacking having to justify why they were driving their car down the 'wrong' street. Only victims of rape are so intimately scrutinized" (p. 4).

The rape frames of victim blaming are created because news coverage reflects the dominant perceptions of race and gender. News frames constructed on rape myths reinforce misconceptions about race and gender (Belknap, 2010) and thus need to be theorized in terms of intersectionality in the media. Rapes of women of color are under-covered and ignored by the media. Crenshaw's (1991) theorization is an instance of how we should be simultaneously responsive to the gendered and raced dimensions of violence and oppression targeting women of color. Her detailed analysis of sexual assault shows that the bodies of women of color are valued according to their race and gender. The press coverage, including in popular magazines, continues to endorse sexist attitudes that condemn women for their rape victimization. Internationally, too, the rape myth frames tend to blame the victims of sexual assault. Alat (2006), in her study of the Turkish media coverage of victims of rape and sexual assault, discusses blame from a linguistic perspective.

We have seen how race becomes an important factor in the creation of rape myths, muting the voices of women of color and also framing rape assailants of color as abnormal. One of the prevalent rape myth frames is abnormality, focusing on the identity discourse, as the suspects are men of color. Such discourse typically attributes animalistic qualities to the suspects, reasserting stereotypes at the intersection of race and gender. In the coverage of the rape of a minor girl in Richmond, Virginia, in 2009, the racial background of the assailants was overtly mentioned twice (Worthington, 2013).

A pertinent question here is whether rape myths are constructed differently when a celebrity is involved. Class and status, like race, also seem to have a similar impact on creating rape myths. Rape myth frames shift considerably when celebrities are suspected of sexual assault. Franiuk et al. (2008) list seven types of rape myth frames that are used when celebrities are involved: (1) she is lying, (2) she asked for it, (3) she wanted it, (4) rape is trivial, (5) he didn't mean to, (6) he's not the type; and (7) it only happens to some women. Rape myths discount the experience of the assault victim and maintain social misperceptions about sexual assault: "Rape myths serve to not only perpetuate misinformation about sexual assault but also prevent communication of accurate information about sexual assault" (Franiuk et al., 2008, p. 301).

Rape myth frames also stigmatize women who have been raped or sexually assaulted. The media in many countries are legally bound to withhold the name of the assaulted woman, as is the case in India, to protect her honor. This stigmatizes rape and objectifies the body of the woman. "The stigma associated with rape remains grave for rape victims and all too often impedes victims coming forward. Therefore, the cases that do come forward in the legal system tend to be the same sort of cases that the media deem . . . newsworthy. And these are most frequently the more unusual and the more sensational types of rape cases" (Ardovini-Brooker & Caringella-Macdonald, 2002, p. 4). This is true globally. Rape cases and sexual assault are not uncommon in India. However, the Delhi gang-rape case of 2012[2] became sensational and received prolonged national and international coverage. The brutality associated with the case made it unusual, leading to mass protests and, eventually, a change in the existing law. Media frames and coverage of sexual assault address patriarchal concerns like the perils of a woman working outside the confines of the home, issues of safety in urban spaces, and preserving the "honor" of the women and their families. What was not in the purview of Hegde's (2011) study was what the media failed to address in this coverage. I speculate that the print media refrained from addressing the concerns and expectations of women as individuals, not as part of a patriarchal family structure. Hegde writes that the coverage was male-centric, which is not a surprise, as men control the majority of the newsrooms. Although women have gained a foothold in news journalism, they are stuck at the bottom (with notable exceptions). Men still control the decision-making process (Ross & Carter, 2011).

But how does the audience decode the rape myths? To me, this seems like asking which came first, the chicken or the egg? Through feminist media theorization, we are trying to decipher whether audience perception encourages the rape myth frames or whether the rape myth frames reinforce the audience's opinion. Worthington's (2008) multimodal study of the encoding and decoding of rape and sexual assault examines the construction of rape by the news media and its reception by the audience. Worthington highlights the differences between the agenda of the news producers and its reception by the audience with regard to understanding news of rape: the audience (mostly women) perceived reporting on rape as a form of advocacy, although that was not the sentiment shared by the newsroom.

The discussion of rape myths is tied to societal perceptions. However, we need to assess whether the newsroom dynamics and gender gap influence the skewed coverage of rape and sexual assault. The rape reform movement, starting in the 1970s, fought against the "double victimization" of rape victims—first by the rapist and then by the media—and helped in broadening the definition and coverage of rape in the media (Ardovini-Brooker & Caringella-Macdonald, 2002). There is scholarship on the issue-based reporting of sexual assault and coding of sexual assault news in order to understand journalism production practices and values. In order to maintain objectivity and balance, the press provides equal prominence and coverage to the perpetrators' voices, eventually relegating the victim's story to lesser importance (Meyers, 2004). Ironically, rape gets more media attention than do other issues related to women. However, this attention is often superficial because the media focus is on the events and not on the process or subtext that led to the incidence of rape and sexual assault (Hegde, 2011).

To increase readership, newspaper editorial staff, who are primarily men, exploit news about rape and sexual assault. The newsworthiness of women comes from whether they are adhering to the cultural norms of femininity or violating them. Women are stereotyped in the news as participants in adultery, infidelity, abduction, love affairs, and domestic violence, as good or bad mothers, or as visual material in criminal cases committed by their male partners, putting the blame on the women rather than on the men who are committing the crimes. This leads us to another question: Does the gender of the newsroom editor influence the coverage in any way? Past research indicates that stories are assigned to reporters based on their gender (Craft & Wanta, 2004). This has two outcomes: more women in newsroom management could lead to increased coverage of women's issues and a decrease in stereotyping of women. However, the question remains as to what are women's issues, and whether bringing a women's perspective to other news is limited (Craft & Wanta, 2004):

> First, newspapers with a high percentage of women in managerial positions tended to cover news in a more positive light. This could be due to male-dominated newsrooms continuing to adhere to traditional news values that emphasize conflict or "bad" news. The old cliché "if it bleeds, it leads" is reflected in the findings. Indeed, crime news was an important aspect of news coverage across all newspapers, but particularly so at newspapers with mostly male editors, according to these findings. Second, female and male reporters tended to cover a similar agenda of issues only when they worked for newspapers with a high percentage of women in managerial positions. (p. 135)

Does the aggressive work culture in the newsroom have an impact on journalistic reporting on rape? I am not confident of the answer here, but past research on newsroom values indicates that both males and females in the newsroom internalize the hegemonic values and behavior of men (Everbach, 2006). Alat (2006) argues that it is unrealistic to expect that in male-dominated newspapers, female writers, except for a few, would show sensitivity to issues of violence against women. Elmore's (2007) study of women journalists who had quit their jobs in newsrooms discusses how they were appreciated at work only when they behaved like one of the "boys." Women not only have to internalize male hegemonic behavior, but they also have to endure constant professional scrutiny with respect to whether they are getting ahead using their sex and sexuality (Everbach, 2006). Masculine news values take priority as the principal news value and are reflected in certain norms in the practice of journalism. Elmore (2007) describes how masculine and patriarchal news values are practiced in the newsroom through exclusionary strategies (golfing, drinking, etc.) and being tough and unemotional.

The following is an excerpt from Geertsema's (2009) interview with Robin Morgan, former editor in chief of *Ms.* magazine and the current global editor, in which she explains the publication's policy as follows:

> It is *Ms.* policy that (whenever and wherever possible) coverage on women in other countries will be done by feminist reporters from/of those countries, so as

to avoid—however well-intentioned—insensitivities and errors on the part of "outsider" journalists. Over the years, we've found that this makes an enormous difference in coverage. There is simply no way (especially regarding stories from the Global South) that a visiting, outside journalist, no matter how sympathetic, can approximate the depth, cultural knowledge, context, nuance, even language, of a national. Furthermore, this gives local and "indigenous" women journalists a chance to publish in *Ms.*—which gladdens their hearts (and our readers) (interview conducted on May 19, 2005).

As seen in the above paragraph, recognizing intersectional identities and engaging in transnational feminist theorization in the media support the inclusive theorization of feminism in the media.

ANALYSIS OF SEXUAL ASSAULT DISCOURSE IN THE NEWS (JOURNALISM)

Sexual assault discourse in journalism is shaped by media censorship and the framing of the incidents. Journalism scholars note the dichotomy in reporting on sexual assault—on the one hand, there is censorship of reportage on rape and sexual assault; on the other hand, the limited coverage includes sexualization and victimization of the woman (Dreze & Sen, 2013; Joseph, 2008; Rao, 2014). Dreze and Sen (2013) theorize that rape is common in India, but the coverage of sexual violence has been limited in Indian media (p. 226). Rao (2014) and Joseph (2008) reveal that the Indian media fail to address the complicated background against which the discourse on sexual assault or rape operates. Rao (2014) extends the discussion of feminist scholars of rape to the different circumstances in which they operate in India: "Feminist scholars have written at length about the prevalence of rape in Indian society—for instance, describing the incidents of mass rape during the partitioning of India in 1947, during which at least 100,000 women were raped, or the events that transpired in 1972 during the war of Bangladesh, when another 200,000 women were reportedly raped by the Pakistani army (Butalia, 2000). . . . Indian laws have been unclear about 'sex without consent' (Bhattacharjee p. 31), often blatantly ignoring or condoning sexual violence against wives and family members" (Rao, 2014, p. 160)

Journalism scholars writing on sexual abuse also theorize transnational feminism and media representation. This not only stigmatizes rape but also objectifies the body of the woman. Mahr (2013) points out that the media should reconsider withholding the name of the raped woman to eliminate the culture of shame associated with rape.

Journalism scholars such as Rao (2014), Durham (2015), and Hollander and Rodgers (2014) conducted discourse analysis of interviews and newspaper reports. Joseph (2008) based her findings on conducting newsroom ethnography and drawing data from secondary surveys conducted by government and/or nonprofit agencies.

Women's studies scholars such as Bhattacharya (2014) and Chantler and Gangoli (2011) analyze incidents and laws to understand the issues of sexual assault, shaming, and intersectionality. In contrast to the journalism scholars, women's studies scholars also reflect on their own socioeconomic situations throughout the discussion.

Their studies of news frames for rape and sexual assault focus on the spatial and legal politics of rape and sexual assault. They focus on the issue of access to space and the ethics and newsroom politics of rape coverage, recognizing the importance of societal hierarchy and the politics of power in matters concerned with rape (Dey, 2016; Rao, 2014). In the context of increasing oppositional voices, conservative groups are also using social media platforms to create discourses about rape and sexual assault, in a backlash against the oppositional voices.

Yamaguchi (2014), in her work on tracing the trajectory of the term "gender free," uses a myriad of methods—archival research on news media, social media, blogs, and interviews with bureaucrats, journalists, local citizens, and activists— to investigate the backlash. This method helps in the understanding of how rape and sexual assaults against women are discussed in the larger society. To understand the political movement and the backlash related to "gender free," Yamaguchi also interviews conservative editors and policy makers. This demonstrates her ability to include oppositional voices in her research to provide clarity and context to the readers. I have seldom come across this approach in the discipline of journalism.

Rape and sexual assault are not issues and concerns unique to Indian society—irrespective of geographic location, rape and sexual assault of women are a reality. As a heuristic device, rape and sexual assault of women and related content could be located across time and space. Taking a cue from Weinbaum et al. in *The Modern Girl Around the World: Consumption, Modernity, and Globalization* (2008), my analysis will also investigate whether there is a variance in the rape script after the emergence of citizen engagement on social media sites like Twitter. Weinbaum makes use of "connective comparison" in her research by analyzing texts to identify the similarities in the representation of the modern girl in the global context (p. 26). In the present context, the news media are not the only source of information; social media as the public sphere also plays an equally important role. I decided to choose both types of media to represent a comparative analysis of discussions of rape in the public sphere.

My experience of being a journalist and of having dealt with reports of sexual assault influenced me in my investigation of the rape script discourse. Victimization, the culture of shaming, and victim blaming create media representations of rape as an individual responsibility. Structural issues of gender insensitivity and the skewed sex ratio are ignored in news reports. There needs to be social and political engagement to create gender sensitivity with regard to rape and sexual assault, which should also be extended to the newsroom. The public needs to be sensitized regarding gender issues, and information plays a key role in achieving this. My goal is to help stir the discussion of rape scripts and encourage the creation of neutral reporting on sexual assault through my scholarship and activism efforts. Many might consider my identity as an insider as a limitation, but I consider my identity and experience to be an asset that has allowed me to make inroads into the small and closed community of Indian media and conduct meaningful research for the public good.

I would argue that there is no one single feminist media theory; feminist media theories include the various feminist theories that emanated from the waves of the feminist movement. Feminist theorizing of media is increasingly overcoming the limitations of its focus on a particular demographic. On the whole, feminism is embracing newer paradigms to accommodate activism and theorizing. "The feminist project is becoming increasingly inclusive of many kinds of differences, including among women and across feminist theorizing" (Steiner, 2013, p. 116). The feminist theorizing of the media now includes the fluid understanding of intersectional identity. This fluidity of intersectionality and transnational feminism has enhanced feminist media theorization beyond the Western-focused feminist media studies. The feminist theorization of the media is a constantly evolving framework owing to the shifts in communication and media studies. Gallagher (2007) writes that the scholarship of feminism in media studies has sustained itself by combating the changes in the profession and the discipline: "The development of the media industries themselves presents constant and ever more complex problems for feminist scholarship. Yet feminist media criticism survives, despite the regular appearance of 'postfeminist' arguments and the onslaught of more overt backlash" (p. 35). There is a greater scope for research on the evolving feminist perspective on media. We need to raise our sisterhood, along with our intersectional identities of race, class, citizenship, and religion, to coalesce in our struggle against patriarchal norms within the media and foster feminist media theorizing in our scholarship.

FROM THE LENS OF THE CONCEPT OF INTERDEPENDENT AGENDA BUILDING

Figure 2.1, a model of interdependent agenda-building concept, will support the engagement of grassroots feminist activists and journalists for anti-rape and sexual harassment activism. There has been an increased focus by the media and by online feminist campaigns on the issues of rape and sexual assault in India (Gangoli & Rew, 2015); however, the conviction data indicate that they are not having enough of an impact on policy makers to effect widespread changes in policy. There has been no sustained media campaign on the implementation of

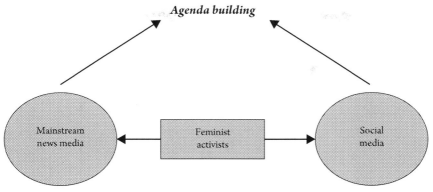

FIGURE 2.1. Interdependent agenda-building model

policies such as rape crisis centers, fast-track courts, or the provision of rehabilitation or security for the victims (Himabindu et al., 2014). Social media has fostered a sense of hybrid protest (where social media pressure fosters more traditional media attention), and the interdependence of both could build social capital to tackle the issue of violence against women with impunity more broadly.

The rise of the internet and social media sites has given a new direction to feminist activism in India, where women share their experiences of street and sexual harassment (Dey, 2014; Eagle, 2015). According to Eagle (2015), "Hashtag activism is part of the important work of awareness-raising, contributing to a larger conversation about eve-teasing—a practice that, with silence, is allowed to continue unquestioned and under the guise of simply being a part of the culture" (p. 350). Similarly, Dey (2014) highlights the manner in which feminists are using social media to circumvent gatekeeping by the mass media. She argues that online spaces have "helped organizations and individuals to be less dependent on the established mass media in conveying their messages to a broader audience base. The action and reaction followed each other in very short cycles, and the speed of diffusion of new ideas, tactics, and arguments considerably increased. The Internet and social media have also been used to generate useful debates and meaningful conversations related to gender" (p. 200).

Nevertheless, the spurt in online feminist activism in India is not without challenges from trolling, harassment of activists, cybervigilantism, and loss of focus on the core issues of feminist struggles. For instance, the 2012 Delhi gang-rape protests were overwhelmed by demands for violent punishment, such as chemical castration, the death penalty, and stoning, for the perpetrators and others implicated in the rape (Dutta & Sircar, 2013; Losh, 2014; Roy, 2015). In the process, the voices of the Indian feminists who oppose the death penalty were lost in this digital conundrum (Dutta & Sircar, 2013). Losh (2014) chronicled the online narrative after Jyoti Singh's rape and murder, which included hashtags such as #inhumanebastards, #death4rape, and others indicating anger and eagerness for revenge. According to Dutta and Sircar (2013):

> Feminist voices have been a part of these protests, but the chorus of slogans made it difficult to decipher who was saying what. There were loud calls to end state apathy on violence against women, make public transportation safe, make the police more vigilant, speed up judicial prosecutions, amend rape laws, and stop victim-blaming. But demands for the death penalty, chemical castration, and death by stoning of rapists were louder. . . . In the face of the grave loss, anger, and trauma that gave rise to demands for revenge, how would feminist "rational" political reasoning stand its ground? How were we to converse with the parents who demanded the death penalty for the rapists who had brutally tortured, raped, and murdered their twenty-three-year-old daughter? (p. 295)

Apart from cybervigilantism, there was also the issue of the confusion of activism with popular Bollywood movies. For instance, during the protest movement of the 2012 Delhi gang rape, hashtags such as #braveheart and #Jagruti (awareness) were also trending with #Nirbhaya, but these hashtags were names of Bollywood movies shared by movie fans, creating confusion within the movement. Losh (2014) also points out how the online feminist activists failed the hashtag test in India: "Hashtags must be simultaneously short, unique, memorable, unambiguous in meaning, resistant to variant spellings, and descriptive as content labels. Yet all of the hashtags regularly used by Breakthrough and Blank Noise13 invariably fail at least one of these tests." After the gang rape of Jyoti Singh, #Nirbhaya became the trending hashtag on Twitter from December 2012 to January 2013 (Chopra, 2014; R. Guha, 2015). In a country where social media platforms are limited to only 12 percent of the population (Velayanikal, 2016), a digital divide and lack of digital literacy constitute significant issues. In this situation, developing a bridge between mainstream media and social media activism is important.

The Role of Rural Anti-rape Feminists

Rural and subaltern anti-rape and sexual assault feminist activists work with limited resources and little to no digital training. The inclusion of the rural feminist activists in this book will be enlightening because their perspective is different from the popularly shared version of urban feminist activism in India, which is a subject of constant focus by scholars and writers.

The role and functioning of Indian nonprofits are very different from those of their counterparts in Western countries (Nagar, 2010). Indian nonprofits are hierarchized and have often discriminated against field workers, as has been documented by the Sanghtin writers (a group of subaltern women working as field officers in nongovernmental organizations) in their diaries. When I was trying to recruit activist participants for the interviews, I faced similar hierarchical gate-keeping from some of the nonprofits. I was refused any contact with the field workers, and only the founder/president wanted to meet. When the office of the founder/president called to reschedule the appointment, I asked if I could go and observe the field workers and see how they worked during the meeting. Not only was my request denied, but I was told categorically that the meeting was to be only with the founder/president and no one else—of course, the meeting was never scheduled! Rural feminist activists have come across gatekeeping and barriers while trying to use social media platforms such as Twitter and Face-book. Most prefer to use WhatsApp and still try to use Facebook to build an agenda and network with journalists.

The rural feminist activists have a collegial relationship with the journalists. The rural feminist activists in this study were enlightening for me as a researcher. Not only were they more forthcoming, but they offered a perspective different from the popularly shared version of feminist activism. WhatsApp and Face-book Messenger work much like text services, which is easier for rural feminist activists to use, and they do not have to deal with open social media platforms like Facebook. Facebook pages need constant updates and engagement with the audience; many rural feminist activists do not have access to Facebook. Even if some of these activists did have a Facebook account, they are not proficient in the use of social media platforms. They mostly depend on their family members or digital media professionals to deliver their content to the public and journal-ists through Facebook. Therefore, it is easier for rural feminist activists to com-municate through closed platforms like WhatsApp and other texting services that are easier to navigate. Threatening feminist activists and rape victims is a common practice in rural areas in India, irrespective of the state. Kavita of Khabar Lahariya, Usha of Red Brigade, and Sampat of Gulab Gang narrated inci-dents in which they or the rape victims were threatened by political leaders or the police. In contrast, rural feminist activists restrict themselves to using social media platforms like WhatsApp and Facebook Messenger to network with jour-nalists and, sometimes, policy makers. Most rural feminist activists I interviewed have a smartphone, but there are issues of network connectivity, creating con-tent, and accessing social media platforms like Facebook.

3 · THE HEART DOES NOT BLEED FOR EVERYONE
Selective Outrage and Activism

Conversations with anti-rape and sexual harassment activists and, later, the journalists who spearheaded #MeTooIndia in 2018 revealed that their paths to activism began with personal experiences, and this activism eventually became political. Sandhya, who started the #MeTooIndia movement in 2018, shared that she identifies as both a journalist and an activist because the roles overlap, and journalism is a tool for change. It was Sandhya's tweets and an open call on Twitter in which she asked women who had been sexually harassed or assaulted in the news industry and other workplaces to share their experiences that began the movement. She started by sharing her own.

SEXUAL ASSAULT ACTIVISM IS PERSONAL AND POLITICAL

I spoke with Sutapa, and have been speaking with her on and off since 2016. She is a rural anti-rape and sexual harassment activist working in the interior of Sagar island, empowering women and girls to fight against sexual harassment. Sutapa said, "The girls are harassed at school; if they complain, their parents prevent them from going to school. So, there were times when the girls would just stop complaining. But I teach them and work with them to make them aware that it's not their fault and protest and organize themselves." Sutapa believes things are changing because social media brings the world closer together.

Many miles away in the capital city of Delhi, Dyuti, a young feminist activist, shared a similar personal narrative. A month after the 2012 Delhi gang rape, Dyuti's best friend in college was sexually assaulted in Delhi. When Dyuti's friend filed a police complaint, the politically well-connected perpetrator threatened Dyuti and her friend with an acid attack. Acid attacks are a common tactic in India to scare and threaten women who protest against an assault or defy the

46

patriarchy. Acid is poured on the faces and bodies of women to disfigure them as punishment for spurned sexual advances or to settle scores (Islam, 2016).

Dyuti's friend was forced to withdraw her complaint because of political pressure and fear of an acid attack. Dyuti told me: "I had never felt so helpless. We had joined the protests at Jantar Manter against the Delhi gang rape, but couldn't do anything when we were threatened and my friend was victimized." After this incident, Dyuti joined the autonomous women's cell at her college, Miranda House, and thus took her first step in feminist activism. In India, women's cells have been created in educational institutions, workplaces, and other government institutions to handle complaints related to sexual harassment and to provide a safe working environment for women (UGC guidelines, 2013). Since graduating, Dyuti continues to be actively involved in feminist activism and shares her experiences through social media platforms.

THE POWER OF BEING FACEBOOKISH: SHIFTING THE NARRATIVE ON RAPE AND SEXUAL ASSAULT

Journalists and activists have differing opinions on the coverage of rape and sexual assault in India. Scholars (Belair-Gagnon, Mishra, & Agur, 2014; Phillips et al., 2015; Poell & Rajagopalan, 2015) have focused on social media platforms and their function as a tool for gathering and disseminating information on incidents of rape and sexual assault. However, most of my interviewees pointed out that audiences use social media platforms to monitor journalists with respect to how they frame rape and sexual assault news stories.

After social media platforms became popular in India, journalists began to be called out by social media users for their stereotypical framing of the victims. It has also become easier for journalists to seek information on social media platforms to report on cases.

According to Sayantanee, a former journalist, "Social media platforms create pressure, help us to follow up a case till it reaches some logical end." Citizen engagement on social media sites keeps up the pressure on journalists to report on cases of rape and sexual assault. Sandip, a Delhi-based journalist, agreed with Sayantanee: "In the recent past, journalists think twice before casting aspersions on the character of the victim. I definitely think there is less questioning by the media of the victim's character due to the stress of being called out publicly on social media platforms."

Gyanesh*,[1] a journalist who works for a leading English newspaper in Kolkata, said, "There is no denying that social media has changed the way we journalists cover rape and sexual harassment. This change has been visible since 2012 in the coverage; we focus on the crime that has happened and definitely avoid the 'victim-blaming' questions like what was she wearing and why was she out at night." Chinmay*, a blogger and journalist from Guwahati, corroborated

Gyanesh's comments, saying, "We don't want to get called out on social media and hence the shift. Even though I agree, it's marginal."

Debamoy, a senior journalist in Kolkata, agreed, saying, "After Nirbhaya's gang rape in 2012, and the gang rape of the young schoolgirl in Kamduni in 2013, there has been an awareness in newsrooms that such news needs more focus. Rape or molestation used to get smaller spaces. They became important in 2012. I can share from my individual experience; there has been a change in the newsroom. Even in 2005, there would many cases of rapes and sexual assault and harassment the districts, but senior editors [would either not carry the news or they would relegate the news to smaller space on inside pages]. But social media has been a big help, and people are more 'Facebookish.' The parallel space for news, even in semi-rural areas, has been one of the reasons for the focus on rape and sexual harassment news. I can't deny that the newsrooms are cautiously trying to understand the pattern."

INCREASING NUMBERS, DECREASING DEPTH

Sandhya agrees that there has been a shift in the number of news reports on crimes against women, but thinks that the depth of coverage is still low. "There is a quantitative shift, not qualitative, it's kind of a kneejerk reaction; more newspapers are covering the rape and sexual assaults, but there is hardly any follow-up or fine-tuning of language. More neutral words need to be used; for instance, the words 'alleged' and 'claimed.' I have a problem with them because of the loathing that the woman receives. It makes her sound like a liar! Then, the intermingling of sexual harassment and sexual assault is also disturbing."

Recent scholarship also supports this trend. In "If It Bleeds It Leads," authors Andelsman and Mitchelstein (2019) note that, although there has been a quantitative increase in articles on sexual assault, there is a clear lack of analysis in the news stories. Shah (2018) similarly found that there has been a rise in the episodic framing of sexual assault and rape in India after 2012. Although slowly and gradually, some coverage has been focusing on thematic analysis, with respect to the thematic framing of rape and sexual assault coverage in India. This lack of thematic analysis relegates rape and sexual assault to the status of an urban rather than a rural issue (P. Guha, 2017; Shah, 2018).

Noopur also agrees: "Nirbhaya pushed the conversations into the mainstream news media in India; it was problematic, but it brought these conversations into the light. Yes, there have been changes in storytelling but not in concrete action measured for the #MeToo." Noopur teamed up with her collaborators, including Christina Dhanaraj, to run Smashboard, a digital platform for working against sexual abuse and for women's empowerment.

Most journalists agree that follow-up media coverage on rape and sexual assault has been an issue. Diganta said, "Considering the fast turnaround of news in the 24-hour cycle, it is becoming increasingly difficult to do follow-ups in rape and sexual assault news, and it slips away from public memory, conversation, and the agenda. The follow-up happens in some rapes like Nirbhaya's rape, or that of Suryanelli, either due to their extreme brutality or the scandal."

LOCATION, LOCATION, LOCATION: INTERTWINING WITH CASTE AND CLASS

Sexual harassment in nonprofits that fight for the rights of sexual assault survivors and rehabilitate them is not uncommon. Divya* has been working in the nonprofit sector with grassroots activists on sexual assault, harassment, and abuse. She was sexually harassed and assaulted at the nonprofit where she worked. The #MeTooIndia campaign brought back all the memories of the harassment and how the organization was complicit in the cover-up. Divya said, "I quit Twitter after #MeTooIndia. I just couldn't take the information overload, as it reminded me of my experiences. I could share the harassment details, name and shame the perpetrator, but what then? What is the path after naming and shaming? I agree with the movement, but it cannot end just at naming and shaming. Like the implementation of the POSH Act[2] in organizations and legally supporting the survivors."

Divya and I spoke multiple times from 2016 to 2019 about the role of the news media and social media in anti-rape and sexual harassment activism. In 2016 and 2017, Divya shared that the nonprofit organization she worked for did not want to work on sensitive issues such as brothel eviction because it perceived the issue as political and wished to avoid getting its hands dirty or ending up in conflict with the government. Divya decided to move on to another organization after witnessing that resources for survivors were spent on appeasing the government and stakeholders or on luxuries for the senior employees.

In 2019, we spoke again about #MeTooIndia, the impact of social media activism on the rural activists, and more. Divya shared that her understanding of the hashtag movement was that it was elitist because it gives a voice to survivors who have access to resources, which are amplified by the news media. Divya said,

> The rural anti-rape feminist activists have been working on spreading awareness and working against sexual harassment at the grassroots level in rural communities. I work with a Dalit anti-rape feminist activist in Haryana; she accompanies Dalit and lower-caste victims of sexual assault and harassment to the police station to lodge complaints—otherwise, they will be molested and harassed. But neither the social media platforms nor the news media share her #MeTooIndia experience, and the public is not even aware of it. This mobilization has been present but not under any Twitter handle. The importance of anti-rape and sexual harassment activism is locational—the more urban it is, the more popular it becomes.

Noopur, sharing similar concerns, said, "Pushing survivors and congratulating them and identifying them could be dangerous, as some people have the privilege of being identified and dealing with the repercussions, but not all victims are able to deal with the ramifications. And often we don't even know how they are going through. I am wary of the heroism that is attached to the survivors. We need to prepare ourselves and individual efforts, and we feel there has to be a concerted effort."

The experiences of rural and Dalit activists have been missing from the social media narrative until recently. One of the rural activists cited an incident near her village in which a senior nonprofit official sexually harassed a female grassroots worker. When her colleagues protested and a local feminist newspaper reported the incident, there was a strong backlash from the organization. At the behest of the senior official, the nonprofit expelled the female grassroots worker and others who supported her. Nonprofit workers are sometimes dissatisfied with the practices of their organizations. More recently, one of the feminist activist participants left the organization because of the gatekeeping and hierarchy, where the money is spent on five-star accommodations for the nonprofit executive leadership, but field workers are denied the resources they need.

Speaking about #MeTooIndia and its impact in rural Bengal, Debamoy shared, "It did rock the news industry to an extent but had negligible to no impact on the larger public sphere, especially in rural West Bengal." Sutapa agreed, commenting, "The girls and women who work with me are on Facebook and WhatsApp—they see, read, and hear what others are posting on sexual assault, but they don't post any of their opinions or experiences. No doubt it encourages them in some form—there is awareness of what is happening in the world but in their immediate community, there is no impact of the hashtags."

In this book, I have included location as an important factor in intersectional identity, along with caste, class, and religion. Previous research in India and other countries has identified the intersectional identity of the victim in rape and sexual assault cases as an important factor in media coverage (P. Guha, 2015; Shah, 2018). News frames that are constructed based on rape myths reinforce misconceptions regarding race and gender (Belknap, 2010). Rapes of women of color are under-covered and ignored by the media. In India, women belonging to the minority segments have a similar experience when their rape is covered by the media. Crimes against Dalit women, other lower-caste women, lower-class women, and women belonging to minority religions have less visibility in the media (Shah, 2018). Amit*, a senior journalist working for an English newspaper, said, "A molestation or alleged rape that occurred in a slum by shanty dwellers will usually not get much coverage or any coverage at all. Editors frequently brush them aside as being not newsworthy. But such an allegation in a high-profile or social elite class family will attract huge attention. It is mainly on the profile of the victim and nature of the crime."

Selective Outrage and Activism   51

The prominence of the location is important in the follow-up of the rape coverage. To understand the significance of the role that location plays, I analyzed three rapes and murders: those of Pratibha in Bangalore in 2005, Jyoti in New Delhi in 2012, and Jisha in Perumbavoor (Kerala) in 2016.[3] The prominence of the location creates a hierarchy in the framing of the location, forming a prejudiced response in the public and among policy makers. Gyanesh had covered Jyoti's rape and murder for his publication and candidly shares, "I am very doubtful that Nirbhaya's rape and murder would have made the same impact and coverage if she was found even five-six kilometer away from the city center. It is unfortunate but true that the coverage and the outrage would have been much less."

Of course, incidents of rape or sexual harassment in urban areas in India get much more media attention; however, most scholarly work on the media coverage of rape in India—correctly—focuses on the intersections of class, caste, and religion (Fadnis, 2017; Jolly, 2016, Virmani, 2016). Hardly any value has been given to location in either scholarly discussions or media critiques. The coverage also did not address the issue of location-based biases that often guide the amount of coverage that a rape incident receives. Other journalists and activists also agreed that the location of the incident influences its coverage. With this feedback, I looked for the kind of coverage that "location" received—even when location did come up in the coverage, it was framed in terms of "small towns," "posh areas," and "important localities."

I looked for specific references to the locations of the incidents; the importance of the location in the interviews with and quotes from citizens, elites, and celebrities; and finally, how the location was framed by the journalists. In Pratibha's case, an article jointly published in the *Times of India* and the *Economic Times* emphasized the safety measures in the metropolitan cities of India: "Something like this can happen anywhere in India, but I don't think it's a big threat to us in Mumbai. It is definitely no issue for us, but it's the higher-ups who have to worry. . . . When a car enters the Hi-Tech city (Hyderabad's IT hub), there are security personnel at the entrance that check each and every car. What's more, when we enter the Nipuna building, we are checked with metal detectors and are frisked as well. Most employees in Mumbai feel that the attacks in Bangalore are of no consequence" (Vyas, 2005).

There was a repeated focus on big cities and the security and infrastructure available in those cities, as well as on how the rest of India is different from the major cities. When the rape and murder of Jyoti was reported on, the focus was on Delhi, framed as the nation's capital. As Nandi (2012) noted, "It is our complacency that has led to this situation. Delhi is the rape capital because such crimes are normalized after a few days. Criminals get away, and Delhiites go back to being complacent."

Similarly, the following coverage justified calling Delhi the rape capital: "Delhi has earned the odium of the 'rape capital' with an incidence of 572 rape cases in 2011. But in the same year, it is Madhya Pradesh that reported the highest number of cases for rape (3,406), molestation (6,665) and importation of girls (45) accounting for 14.1%, 15.5% and 56.3% of the respective national totals" (Mitta, 2012).

Some articles focused on the status of the city being a rape capital, as in this article: "In a new low for a city already notorious as India's rape capital, a 23-year-old physiotherapy student was left battling for her life after being brutally beaten up and raped by at least five drunken men in a private bus which was audaciously driven around south Delhi localities on Sunday night even as the crime was being committed inside" (Chauhan, Ghosh, & Shekhar, 2012).

There were also insinuations that while such an incident might occur in a village or rural area, it was unacceptable in the power corridor of New Delhi. As one article put it, "The incident continued for 90 minutes not in a village or some jungle but in south Delhi" ("Hyderabad Rises," 2012). Similarly, policy makers were concerned only with the safety of women in the capital rather than any others in the country: "Meanwhile, home minister Sushil Kumar Shinde said in Parliament that a special committee, headed by the home secretary, has been constituted to look into the safety of women in Delhi" ("Delhi Gang Rape Case," 2012).

The coverage also emphasized the reactions of the citizens of the location, as in the following example: "The rape triggered nationwide outrage and bringing thousands of Delhiites onto the streets to protest the incident and highlight how loopholes in the legal system allow rapists to go scot-free" ("Hyderabad Rises," 2012).

The coverage was very detailed, describing the exact location of the crime and the follow-up of the crime. Dwaipayan Ghosh noted in his December 23, 2012, article in the *Times of India* that "police are scanning call details of the officials posted between the stretch of Vasant Vihar and Mahipalpur to find out their location on that night. They will also be looking at the logbook details for any dereliction."

There was repeated focus on the prominence of the location. As the country's capital and a metropolis, Delhi was seemingly more important than other parts of the country. Pranjal Baruah stated in his December 20, 2012, article in the *Times of India*: "If a girl is not safe in the national capital, what can we expect from other states? We believe that security forces need to improvise to deal with growing India. Even in Assam, women work till late at night and need to travel alone these days. However, without strict police patrolling and bolstering the women's police wing, the question of women's safety is a distant dream. Where was the patrolling party of Delhi Police when the girl was being tortured in a moving bus?"

Such a detailed description of the location was not seen in either Pratibha's or Jisha's rape and murder coverage. Other coverage questioned the infrastructure and facilities in Delhi and assumed that girls and women ought to be safer in big, metro cities: "This is a shocking case. We condemn the incident. If women are not safe in the national capital, where will they go?" ("Delhi Gang Rape Case," 2012).

In comparison, after Jisha was raped and murdered in 2016, the focus was on the small- town location in another part of the country. In some articles, the location was not specifically identified; instead, it was just referred to as a small town near the state capital, Kochi. "It also comes at a time when Delhi is witnessing protests over the rape-murder of a 29-year-old Dalit law student in a small town near Kerala's Kochi last week" ("Kerala Woman," May 2, 2016).

The following is another example: "Two men were detained on Tuesday for the brutal rape-murder of a 29-year-old Dalit law student in a small town near Kerala's Kochi last week, a crime that drew comparisons with the Delhi 2012 gang rape" ("Kerala Woman," May 2, 2016).

Other articles identified the location where Jisha was raped and murdered, but they immediately drew parallels with Jyoti's rape and murder in New Delhi: "A 30-year-old Dalit law student was raped and murdered on April 28 in Perumbavoor, Ernakulam, Kerala. The incident sparked condemnation in the country with many drawing parallels with the 2012 Nirbhaya case in New Delhi" ("Social Justice Minister," 2016).

Some articles focused on the reasons why geographical location mattered in the coverage of rape and sexual assault: "There was widespread outrage over the Nirbhaya case because every urban woman could relate to it" (Aneja, 2016).

Even now, after #MeTooIndia happened, it was the urban and semi-urban women who were part of the conversation, not the rural women. There has been limited focus on the rural women, as well as limited conversation about them. Chandola (2018) rightly observes that the #MeTooIndia movement has had a limited reach in professions and spaces beyond the media, academia, journalism, and other urban professions. In her research, Chandola recognizes the impact of unsafe public spaces, institutionalized violence in unorganized sectors, and the physical and emotional trauma associated with sexual harassment and assault as everyday lived experiences of rural and marginalized women.

Between September 1, 2018, and October 31, 2018, in the *Times of India* (Electronic Edition) and the *Hindustan Times*, 106 articles were published on #MeTooIndia, #MeToo in India, and sexual harassment. Table 3.1 shows the distribution of the articles.

TABLE 3.1.	Distribution of articles, September 1–October 31, 2018
Publication	Number of articles
Times of India	62
Hindustan Times	44

The majority of the coverage from both newspapers focused on the unsafe public spaces in the metropolitan cities and second-tier cities.[4] City-based teachers, citizens, and others who were interviewed for the news stories focused on the need to secure the public spaces for women in urban areas and city college campuses. This focus on the importance of location is hardly a shift from the previous coverage comparing the rapes and murders of Pratibha, Jyoti, and Jisha, and later of the #MeToo movement. Subhro clarifies that most of the papers' readers are city-based, hence the focus on location.

IMPACT OF GATEKEEPING AND HIERARCHY IN ACTIVISM AND COVERAGE

Social media users, scholars, activists, journalists, and the public agree on the existence of gatekeeping at all levels, by individuals, technological platforms, and organizations advertently as well as inadvertently. There is technological gatekeeping, algorithmic gatekeeping, and social gatekeeping, all of which hierarchize anti-rape and sexual harassment activism (Kahn & Kellner, 2012) so that hashtag activism is restricted to a certain group of users with access, literacy, and resources. There is no denying that the internet provides a space for marginalized groups to voice their opinions and construct their activism, but it is not without risks and challenges for the activists, including online stalking, trolling, abuse, and offline surveillance (Brimacombe et al., 2017; Housley et al., 2018).

Hierarchy and gatekeeping within anti-rape feminist activism also impact the movement and its coverage, leading to distrust. Noopur shares her thoughts on this gatekeeping:

> Feminist gatekeepers banished the activists of #LoSHA, and the same people showed reluctance in welcoming activists from the marginalized communities. There is also a hierarchy in the #MeToo movement, depending on whether people are leading them or not, whether it's inclusive or not. This gatekeeping makes the fight against sexual harassment and abuse difficult. Dalit feminists are correcting the course of Indian feminism via social media. And the mainstream news media is taking its cue from the social media platforms. I think acknowledging our privileges, and the praxis of the intersectionality would help us deal with the issues of hierarchy.

Social media networking tools aid and support activism efforts and influence news coverage, but they do not replace actual activism. Harlow and Harp (2012) conducted an exploratory study on the impact of social networking sites on online and offline activism. The results suggested that, despite the digital divide, activists regard internet platforms like Facebook and Twitter favorably. However, it should not be assumed that these digital tools are replacing traditional offline strategies. Harlow and Harp proposed that online and offline actions need to be combined to achieve real social change.

Social Media a Boon, and Sometimes a Bane

Tarun*, an executive editor of a daily newspaper in Goa, highlighted the perils of social media platforms in journalism: "As much as social media is helpful, sometimes it becomes a nuisance in rape or sexual assault coverage. There are instances of circulation of false information, which young journalists circulate without verifying." Similarly, Pratap, an editor of a Hindi newspaper in New Delhi, agreed that any lead from a social media source needs to be thoroughly checked: "There have been many cases in my career that a lead has turned out to be false. The first thing is to check and then see if the victim reported it. Then we try to find the FIR and see what steps have taken place and then report on it. We don't just perform our professional duties as journalists, but we also have a social responsibility, which is helping the public."

Is the role of the journalist changing because of social media platforms? There is emerging scholarship on the amalgamation of the roles of journalists and activists owing to the changing role of social media platforms and the engagement of journalists (Barnard, 2017; Russell, 2016). This intertwining role of journalists and activists is evident from my conversations after the #MeTooIndia movement.

INTERWEAVING ROLES OF JOURNALIST AND ACTIVIST

Much like Sandhya, Noopur of Smashboard thinks that since #MeToo happened, we are witnessing an overlapping of roles between journalists and activists. Noopur is the president and founder of Smashboard, and also a journalist. According to Noopur, "There is an overlap of roles as a journalist and activist, and it's difficult to differentiate. And this concept came into being around 2016, specifically after the social media movements."

Kavita and Sayantanee also like to identify themselves as both journalists and activists. However, there is a clear gender difference in this identification. Male journalists do not identify themselves as activists or do not see their roles as overlapping—for instance, both Gyanesh and Debamoy said their primary role is reporting the news, not engaging in activism. Others, in fact, were wary of being associated with activists and not journalists. As I identified earlier, much of the activism is sparked by a personal experience, so female journalists, having faced sexual harassment at work comparatively more than male journalists, often see themselves as more involved in the interweaving role of activism and journalism (N. Khan, 2018). The changing role of social media platforms and their impact on news media platforms has also been a contributing factor in this new role that journalists have found for themselves (Blanding, 2018).

After the #MeTooIndia movement gained ground on Twitter and Facebook, a crowdsourced list of lawyers, activists, health professionals, and journalists was created to support the movement. While sharing this list, many journalists were referred to or identified as allies. Adrija Dey, an activist and academic, said, "There are some journalists who are our allies, and immediately identify and pick up the incidents that need the public attention."

Journalism and social movements are increasingly becoming dependent on one another, and not just in the context of anti-rape and sexual harassment activism. Blanding (2018) also writes about this interdependent role: "Even as journalism is overlapping with activism in some ways, some activists are also venturing into journalism."

Rape and Sexual Harassment as a Political Issue

The journalists I interviewed confirmed Jolly's (2016) finding that the coverage of rape and sexual harassment has received more space since 2012. However, they shed light on the fact that rape and sexual harassment are political issues, not merely social issues. Gyanesh, who covered the Delhi gang rape, said: "The activism and protests were due to the dissatisfaction of the citizens with the government of the day. The anti-corruption and graft movement of the citizens had fueled the anti-rape protests. You can say it's an offshoot of the previous protests; there was a tremendous anti-incumbency wave against that government. All these spiraled to make it a bigger issue."

The Kamduni gang-rape case became big because the perpetrators involved were allegedly party members and workers of the ruling party of the state. The then chief minister of West Bengal suspected the rape was the work of the opposition party (Bhadra & Chakrabarty, 2013), which quickly turned it into a political issue. Likewise, whatever coverage the Jisha rape case of Kerala received in 2016 was because of the impending assembly elections in the state.

Diganta agreed with Gyanesh: "Prime Minister Modi spoke about Jisha during his campaign in the context of unsafe public spaces for women, but he did not tweet or write on Facebook about her. I doubt that many people were following the campaign in Kerala. High-profile rape cases become politicized, and political parties take the opportunity to discredit one another."

Not much has changed over the years, Debamoy said, because rape and sexual assault are political tools of oppression, and political clout keeps us from always hearing about it. In 2012 the Park Street rape was politicized; during election years, sexual assault becomes a tool of intimidation.

When the #MeTooIndia movement started again in September 2018, one of the first assertions by some political and social observers was that the movement was politically motivated and orchestrated because one central minister was accused of harassment, which has made the issue controversial.

Debamoy and Gyanesh both agreed that rape and sexual assault are becoming tools to intimidate women. Gyanesh said, "Whether or not the perpetrators would get punished depends on the political, economic, or other clout they have in the larger society. The same holds true for the #MeTooIndia movement and newsroom sexual harassment. There haven't been any real repercussions for the perpetrators."

Sexual Harassment and Rape Still Off-Limits

Police reports on rape and sexual assault in India have been on the rise in the past decade. The National Crime Records Bureau (NCRB) reports a 52.2 percent increase in the incidence of rapes reported from 2002 to 2012. In the case of sexual assault, the increase from 2002 to 2012 has been 33.6 percent. This increase in the reporting of rape and sexual assault continued until 2016. According to the latest data from the NCRB of India, the reporting of incidents of rape and sexual assault increased 12 percent in 2016, after a decrease in 2015 as compared with the previous year

Sexual assaults and rape constitute 4.3 percent of the total percentage share of all crimes (NCRB, 2017). The rate of filing charges (the number of cases investigated that were officially documented) in incidences of rape is 92.1 percent, and sexual harassment is 88.6 percent, which is higher than the rate for crimes of murder (83%), but the conviction rate in cases of rape and sexual harassment has remained dismally low at 23.9 percent for rapes. The conviction rate for murder is 30.0 percent, which is higher than the rate for sexual offenses. The data point to a wide gap between the rate of filing charges of sexual assault against women and the rate of conviction. Victims are encouraged to file a report with the police, but a majority of the offenders are not convicted due to the lack of a proper investigation, the humiliation of victims during the medical and judicial procedures, and the long, drawn-out judiciary proceedings (Himabindu et al., 2014). A Dalit anti-rape feminist activist, based in a village in rural northern India, often faces harassment and rebuke while trying to help rape survivors and victims file police complaints. Prashanti Tiwari, a sexual harassment survivor working at the United Nations, wrote about the obstacles surrounding filing complaints, due diligence, and justice: "The 'zero' cases reported under sexual harassment (PC 354A) by National Crime Records Bureau (NCRB) for Patna in 2016 rather beautifully sums up the experiences of the survivors, who most often, even in the most 'harrowing' cases, do not report the incident to the authorities concerned" (NCRB, 2017).

There has been an increased focus by the media and by online feminist campaigns on the issues of rape and sexual assault in India (Gangoli & Rew, 2015); however, the conviction data indicate that they are not having enough of an impact on policy makers to bring about widespread changes in policy. After the

NCRB report was published, there were multiple news reports on the findings of the report, specifically on violence against women, but there were limited "hashtag" discussions.

More often than not, there is inconsistent follow-up and media coverage of rapes and sexual harassment in India (P. Guha, 2017). Kathryn Clancy (2019), in her keynote at the Faculty Sexual Misconduct Conference, noted in the context of sexual harassment and abuse in academia that the social media and public outrage, along with news media coverage, usually takes place in the case of incidents that are "come-ons," which are severe and treated as outliers, and for which punishment is meted out immediately. "Put-downs" are sexist and sexual harassment, accounting for 92 percent of the total number of incidents (Clancy, 2019); however, it is the come-ons that get the media attention. The come-ons are the tip of the iceberg and usually fail to receive sustained follow-up from either the news media or social media because it involves hostile responses as well, such as trolling and doxing. Sexual harassment and abuse in the form of come-ons and put-downs are outcomes of the existing power structure in any given society.

4 · THE SUCCESSES AND FAILURES OF TRANSNATIONAL HASHTAG MOVEMENTS

This chapter will map the transnational anti-rape and sexual harassment movements worldwide, curate the movement of hashtag anti-rape and harassment feminist movements, and interview the feminist activists on the movement, backlash, and constraints of hashtags on feminist activists who founded these transnational movements. It is also important to note, however, how the agenda around hashtag movements is set and to assess the role of intermedia agenda setting.

The relationship between the various forms of media provides a framework for the intermedia effects of agenda setting. McCombs (2014) provides an example of operationalizing intermedia agenda setting: "The role of elite news in initiating widespread coverage of new topics and the influence of key journalists in framing the news are dramatic examples of intermedia agenda setting. But prosaic versions of intermedia agenda setting take place every day as local news organizations construct their daily agenda from the huge file of news sent to them by the wire services" (p. 129).

Intermedia agenda-setting research has strictly focused on the transfer of salient issues from wire news to newspapers, from newspapers to television networks, and later from newspapers to political blogs. The initial research on intermedia agenda setting was focused on the relationships between daily newspapers and national news agencies. However, this was much before the theorization of agenda setting. B. Lee, Lancendorfer, and Lee (2005) chronicle the history of intermedia agenda setting:

One of the first studies, a case study by White (1949), examined the news selection behavior of a midwestern wire news editor named Mr. Gates. Snider

(1967) showed that there was a strong correlation of news categories between newspaper and wire service in a replication study of the same editor 17 years later. Replicating the Mr. Gates study, McCombs and Shaw (1976) supported the findings of White. Through the replication study of the Mr. Gates study, Hirsch (1977) insisted that the news selection behavior of the news editor was an unconscious reflection of those of the news wire service. Additional research explored the influence of major newspapers on other newspapers and on network television. Roberts and McCombs (1994) extended the concept of intermedia agenda setting to political advertising. (p. 59)

Later, when cable news and network news became prominent sources of news consumption, the intermedia agenda-setting model was applied to television and print media. Sikanku (2011) determined from past research that newspapers followed the agenda set by the wire services (Breed, 1955; Cassidy, 2008). Later research revealed that the agendas of the print media influenced the agendas discussed on television (Borah, 2006; B. Lee et al., 2005).

Scholars such as Walgrave and Van Aelst (2006) focus on the congruence of the different forms of media—they assert that political agenda setting by the media is contingent on and depends on many circumstances, including the form of the media. They question the relevance and influence of different forms of media and comparatively analyze the influence of television vis-à-vis print on policy makers. For the media to have an influence on the political agenda, high compatibility of different media systems is required (Eilders, 2001). However, there are also arguments against intermedia agenda setting. Traditionally, long before the advent of social media, well-known newspapers like the *New York Times* and *Washington Post* were known to have an impact on the reporting of the other media outlets (print, television, and radio). There has also been a manifest impact on political advertising by intermedia agenda setting. Some scholars have challenged the implementation of intermedia agenda setting between web-based media and mainstream mass media. Althaus and Tewksbury (2002) focus their study on the question of whether the print version and the online version of a newspaper share the same perception of political issues, suggesting that the format of mass media influences agenda-setting methods. They found that the agendas of the audience of the printed *New York Times* front page were distinctly different from those of the audience of the online version of the *New York Times*.

Similarly, Groshek (2008) claims that CNN and CNN International Online have the same issue agendas but maintain distinct frames for those issues. This study inquires into whether new media set agendas differently than mainstream media. Online news lets readers choose and structure their news. The results indicate that news personalization has a positive impact on news and issue agenda understanding. B. Lee et al. (2005), in their research on agenda-setting effects on news media and the internet in South Korea, argue that the content of the internet leads public opinion and media coverage. The authors question how the agenda of one type of medium influences the agenda of the other. The main purpose of this study is to investigate the intermedia relationship between the internet and traditional media within the theoretical framework of agenda setting. B. Lee et al. perceive the internet as a public sphere controlled by the public. However, earlier studies on intermedia agenda setting are limited to discussion boards and blogs, which were more popular in the early days of the internet. With the popularity and usability of social media networks, it is worth investigating whether the intermedia effect is true for social media networks and mainstream media. The theoretical scope of the intermedia agenda-setting theory has expanded to the internet across different regions with the rise of new media technologies (Sikanku, 2011).

Other areas of intermedia agenda-setting scholarship include the function of news gathering and issue attention. The news-gathering function and issue attention are distinctly different in web-based media and traditional news media (Meraz, 2009, 2011). The introduction of online versions of newspapers and political blogs facilitates a conditional relationship between the various forms of media. The mainstream mass media functions in a decentralized process in Web 2.0; therefore, it inculcates public and media agendas across a multitude of media platforms. Often, print news media gathers news agendas and issues from social media networks. The same holds true for the network news media, in which issues are identified and discussed based on trending topics on social media networks. This is an emerging development in global journalism. The hashtags #BlackLivesMatter and #SayHerName became dominant discourses in media agenda setting after repeated cases of police brutality against men and women of color in the United States. Social media networks, especially Twitter, have an agenda-setting influence on network news, as well as print news, in the coverage of mass demonstrations. This trend is not limited to North America, as a similar shift has been noticed in international journalism; #IamCharlie and #IWillRideWithYou were intensively debated in the media and by policy makers.

The intermedia agenda-setting relationships between different forms of news media are not limited to just U.S. political campaigns and elections (B. Lee et al., 2005; Ragas, 2014). Past research on intermedia agenda setting demonstrates that elite outlets such as the *New York Times* and others have included diverse social topics like the effects of global warming and the drug problem in the United States, setting the agenda for a public and political discourse (Ragas, 2014). There is evidence of intermedia agenda setting in the international media. Ragas (2014) identifies these examples in his research on the diversity of the intermedia agenda-setting theory:

A study of a 1995 Spanish election found intermedia relationships between two local Pamplona newspapers and the regional television newscast (Lopez-Escobar,

Llamas, McCombs, & Lennon, 1998). Shifting from Europe over to Asia, two studies set in South Korea also found some evidence of intermedia agenda setting among online newspapers and an online wire service (Lim, 2006) and among three major Korean newspaper websites (Lim, 2011). Finally, a recent cross-national study of elite newspaper coverage in 11 countries around the world found that intermedia correlations in the news may occur not just within one country, but rather across media systems in different markets (Du, 2013). (p. 338)

According to B. Lee et al. (2005), the direction of influence between the media agenda and the public agenda has changed in accordance with the level of agenda setting. Internet news subtly influences and alters the public agenda, thereby creating a "collaborative" relationship between mainstream mass media and web-based news media. Nguyen and Western (2006), in their study on the intermedia agenda-setting relationship between traditional media and the internet, indicate a synchronized relationship between the two platforms. They assert that "the historical coexistence of old and new media will continue in the Internet age. At least within the provision of news and information, instead of driving out old media, the Internet will complement them in serving the seemingly insatiable news and information needs among a substantial segment of society." Therefore, there is scholarship on the need and alliance of internet-based media and traditional forms of news media. However, there is still an opportunity for research on the collaborative function of social media networks and traditional mass media in agenda building and agenda setting.

Social media networks are distinctly different from other internet-based media like blogs in setting the agenda. However, these networks have the capacity to influence the functioning of the intermedia agenda setting. Neuman et al. (2014, p. 195) suggest that "social media users are not demographically representative and diverse social media platforms undoubtedly develop local cultures of expressive style which will influence the character of what people choose to say."

IMPLICATIONS OF SOCIAL MEDIA NETWORKS ON AGENDA-SETTING THEORY

Agenda building and agenda setting stem from the idea of reverse agenda setting. The contention between agenda setting and agenda building arises from the constant negotiation between the public agenda building and the media agenda setting. Internet-related developments in the media have complicated the relationship between agenda setting and agenda building. The relationship between the public and the media has been shifting due to the developments in communication technologies (Martin, 2014). Neuman et al. (2014) modified the original McCombs and Shaw model to incorporate the dynamic discussions on virtual public agenda setting and real public agenda-setting efforts. Neuman et al. argue that issue-based agenda setting is multifaceted, with the rise of social media networks and other digital platforms. They ask a pertinent question about who sets the agenda in the digital age, while introducing the concept of the reverse agenda-setting function of new media. Reverse agenda setting is described as the process of setting the public agenda through social network platforms like Twitter and Facebook. Instead of the news media setting and influencing the public agenda, social media networks enable citizens to set the media agenda. Journalists follow the public agenda on social media networks and other web-based media to accumulate information and reproduce it as the media agenda. Reverse agenda setting is profoundly different from intermedia agenda setting, or the transfer of salience from one media organization to another. Reverse agenda setting is the reverse flow of information from the public to mass media (McCombs, 2014; Neuman et al., 2014). Sayre, Bode, Shah, Wilcox, and Shah (2010) suggest that the rise of new media has the potential to result in a reverse flow of information; due to the speed with which social media outlets such as YouTube and Twitter function, they have the ability to influence the agenda of traditional news outlets. Neuman et al. (2014) depict the concept of reverse agenda setting as the growing influence of the networked public: "With a few keystrokes and mouse clicks, any audience member may initiate a new discussion or respond to an existing one with text or audio, or perhaps images and even video. Transmitting requires minimal effort, and once one is digitally equipped, it is virtually costless. To posit that the power of the public agenda has swung from media elites and establishment institutions to the citizenry would be naïve" (p. 194).

But this discussion of reverse agenda setting does not investigate the conditions that impact the digitally connected public in cultivating the public agenda. One possible circumstance of the reverse flow of information is the concept of agenda congestion. Boydstun (2013) formulates this concept based on the idea of competition for space on the media agenda: "Agenda congestion is how clogged or open the agenda is to new items. The scarcity of attention means that issues must compete for space on the agenda" (p. 44). Boydstun's reference to agenda congestion is in the context of media and policy agenda setting; however, I posit that agenda congestion could be a motivation for the public to initiate a discourse on public agenda building on social media platforms. Transfer of issue salience from social media platforms to the mainstream mass media depends on other external social, cultural, political, and economic factors.

Transfer of issue salience from the news media to the public agenda is also a tenet of agenda setting; however, the question is whether the public agenda can always be successfully transferred to the news media through newer technologies like social media networks. McCombs (2014) describes the relationship between social media networks and the agenda-setting process: "The social media issue agenda is too inclusive, a mélange of messages with highly diverse origins. Primary sources of the messages that make up the public issue conversation on social media are the news events of the day, which call attention to a wide variety of topics and issues" (p. 3).

Social media and the news media thus create a strategic alliance in forming agendas. The news media provide support to the social media agenda to narrow the focus of the diverse public agenda and discussion of the extensive public opinion. Messages from digital media, including blogs and social media, and the traditional mass media are not in conflict with one another (J. Lee, 2007). Instead, they have the potential to strengthen the public agenda and reach policy makers through the media. There is scholarship on the role of social media as a component in the agenda-setting process by providing alternative content to traditional media and examining whether social media, with its relative flexibility and speed, can be an effective source for traditional media outlets (Grzywiska & Borden, 2012).

Some scholars provide more "agency" to the news media as compared with other forms of media, consequently undermining the influence of internet-based media like blogs, discussion boards, and others. Andrews and Caren (2010) posit that the news media can shape the public agenda and influence public opinion and elites by drawing attention to movements' issues, claims, and supporters; social media networks cannot set public agendas in a vacuum without the support of mainstream mass media. Andrews and Caren claim that "the media attention helps to define public understanding of a movement itself. Who its leaders are, what it wants, and how it seeks to bring about social change." Similarly, J. Lee (2007) disputes the influence of internet-based agenda setting: "Bloggers cannot be free from general agenda-setting effects because they also are members of the public. Studies suggested that two opposing factors affect blogs' agendas in coverage of public affairs news: dependence and clustering. Dependence should reinforce mainstream media agendas on blogs via agenda setting. Clustering should lead to idiosyncratic, fragmented agendas of blogs confined within their segregated communities" (p. 755). Grzywiska and Borden (2012) have also identified the concern in their research that social media (and user-generated content) would displace mainstream mass media as the leading information source and agenda setter for audiences in the digital age.

What J. Lee (2007) and Andrews and Caren (2010) have overlooked in their studies is that social movements and the public agenda are interrelated due to the social media networks. Evidence from the recent past indicates that social and political movements are generated and induced by social media networks. Internationally, this started with the Arab Spring in 2010, when citizens of Tunisia, Egypt, Libya, and Yemen took to social media networks to organize political movements in their respective countries against the despotic political regimes. Blogs and social media networks played an important role in relaying the message of the political movement from the repressed Arab countries to the world. Mainstream media were tracking social media networks and following political bloggers to understand the public agenda. It is not far-fetched to assert that international mainstream mass media sought the issues from internet-based media (bloggers and social media networks). Other, domestic instances of the influence of social media networks on the mainstream media agenda include the Occupy movement, the Black Lives Matter movement, and the He for She campaign. In spite of this trend, it may be premature to claim that social media networks and blogs will completely eliminate the influence of mainstream mass media in agenda setting. Mainstream mass media have the ability to bring people the public agenda as discussed on social media networks. Therefore, in the present context of communication technology and agenda setting, it would be unreasonable not to consider the contribution of web-based media and focus only on traditional news media to stimulate the public agenda or identify mainstream mass media as the dominant source in setting the agenda. As Grzywiska and Borden (2012) note: "Agendas are attributed to either 'real-world conditions and events' (non-human/nonindividual actors) or 'political actors' (opinion leaders within their respective communities). Intriguingly, though, this definition neglects to consider some of the ways in which power for opinion leadership may have shifted in the social media age" (p. 13).

Recent scholarship on defining the relationship between the internet and agenda setting may challenge the cascading model of top-down information, in which the public merely follows the media agenda, devoid of any ability to influence it. Peterson (2009) challenges this cascading model in her work on the media coverage of terrorism and agenda setting: "The Converse–McGuire Model explains citizen preferences as non-monotonic due to variations in the probability of reception and acceptance: citizens who are moderately aware (receptive) and moderately partisan (acceptant to change) are most malleable for typical events, and the less aware are more malleable for high-intensity messages" (p. 2).

Peterson (2009) employs different models of public opinion: cascading network activation, agenda setting, and the Converse-McGuire model. Agendas range from concrete policy proposals to beliefs and exist at all levels of government and society. The five attributes of the issue-attention cycle are pre-problem, alarmed discovery, realization of costs, decline in density of interest, and post-problem. Peterson correlates media coverage of terrorism along with the issue-attention cycle. However, the research does not investigate whether the diversification of media can lead to diversification of public opinion. Based on Peterson's model, Grzywiska and Borden (2012) theorize that, similar to classical agenda-building theory, Peterson's cycles seem to emerge from the relationship between activity on the social media platforms and mainstream mass media. The Occupy Wall Street movement followed a similar trend when there was scant media coverage at the nascent stage of the movement. However, as political bloggers and social media networks started an online conversation about the movement, there was increased attention from the mainstream mass media.

Similar to the cascading model of information is the concept of agenda control, which speculates that policy-making attention has a significant influence on media agenda/attention. But diversity in discussion impacts the attention and loosens the stronghold of the policy makers (Boydstun, 2013, p. 205). My assumption is that the agenda control is a gatekeeping approach to preserve the elite agenda-setting process with the support of the media. The diversity that Boydstun indicates in her study can be inclusive of the agenda-building efforts through discourses on social media networks.

Impact of Agenda-Building Efforts on Transnational Feminist Digital Movements

The transnational feminist digital movements #Hollaback, #BringBackOurGirls, #TimesUp, #MeToo, and others were created across national boundaries with the help of digital platforms; transnational activists use online platforms to mobilize feminist campaigns (Losh, 2014; Scharff, Smith-Prei, & Stehle, 2016). Transnational movements do not always originate in the Global North; for instance, the #MeToo movement in academia started in India with a crowd-sourced Google list known as #LoSHA. Surprisingly, the #LoSHA movement in India was met with severe backlash from older and renowned feminists in India, and the list was eventually removed. The transnational movements navigate depending on the location, culture, and media systems of the countries. The success of the transnational feminist movements also depends on the political, social, cultural, and economic factors of the particular country; for instance, #MeToo as a movement has been more successful in some countries (such as the United States, the United Kingdom, and, to an extent, Brazil and India) and less successful in others (such as China, Russia, Saudi Arabia, and Indonesia) (Erikson, 2018). It hardly needs repeating that the transnational hashtag movement has not been equally effective everywhere in the world. A year after the movement started in 2017, Karla Adam and William Booth wrote the following in the *Washington Post* on October 5, 2018:

> But for all the early anticipation that things had changed forever, in many countries, the #MeToo movement either fizzled or never took flight.... Women's rights campaigners say that women coming forward and telling their stories can accomplish only so much and that governments and businesses must do more to stamp out harassment. "A year on, we are seeing a lot of people questioning the

movement and whether it's changed anything," said Laura Bates, the British author of *Misogynation: The True Scale of Sexism*."

"Instead," she said, "the question we really need to be asking is: Who takes the baton from the brave survivors who have done such a great service in speaking out?"

There is no doubt that the movement has encouraged many to speak and that many others have passively appreciated it from the sidelines, but the inequity in the transnational digital feminist movement is also seen in the trends and visualization of #MeTooRising, a visualization website created by Google based on the search trends for #MeToo news reports worldwide since October 2017. Figures 4.1–4.3 show that the web searches and news searches for #MeToo mostly occurred in the digital First World countries.

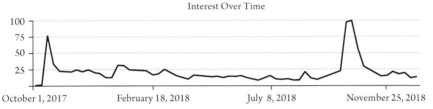

FIGURE 4.1. Worldwide web searches of #MeToo over the nineteen months since the movement started on social media platforms

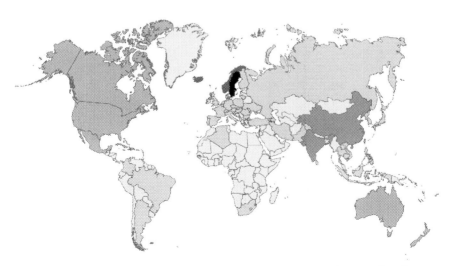

FIGURE 4.2. The global spread of the #MeToo movement since October 2018, based on Google searches

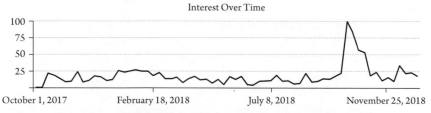

FIGURE 4.3. Global news searches for the #MeToo movement from October 2017 to May 2019

Looking beyond the Internet Mapping

Mapping the transnational movements would give insight into the factors that influence the movement of anti-rape and sexual harassment across country boundaries, and the aspects that influence backlash. An appreciation of the ethics of the feminist movement and the ownership of the term "feminism" in anti-rape and sexual harassment activism helps in understanding the tensions in the transnational feminist movements. Do the transnational digital feminist movements truly reflect inclusivity by including lower-caste, lower-class, and rural and semi-rural anti-rape feminist activists?

Although digital feminist activism has usually been assumed to be a radical political movement of white Western women (Khamis, 2010; Yu, 2009), recent online feminist movements in India suggest that collaboration between feminist movements could culminate in feminist cyberactivism in digitally emerging countries such as India. Examples of transnational feminist collaborations include the SlutWalk, Stop Street Harassment, Hollaback, #LoSHA, and #MeToo movements, which have become prominent in metropolitan cities in India. It is important, however, to remember that these movements are more prominent in the metropolitan cities and other urban and semi-urban areas.

For example, the Facebook page of Hollaback! Mumbai, a transnational movement based on Hollaback!, has been dormant since 2015, unlike the Facebook page of the Hollaback! movement based in New York, which is still engaging with its audience. A network analysis of the Hollaback! Mumbai page and the Hollaback! New York page would prove the difference in the transnational movements and demonstrate the importance of cultural and local contexts in social media–based transnational movements. Movements do have the ability to travel, but their sustainability is based on the local political, economic, and social factors.

To create Figure 4.4, I used Netvizz, a Facebook application that allows downloading of Facebook data (including page network analysis), to identify which types of pages a given page interacts with most. The Hollaback! Mumbai page interacted mostly with local anti-rape and feminist activism pages such as Safecity, Priya's Shakti, Breakthrough India, and a few others.

Transnational Hashtag Movements 69

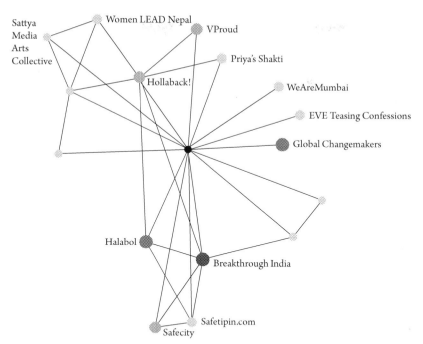

FIGURE 4.4. Network analysis of Hollaback Mumbai!

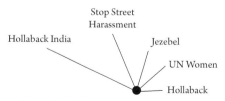

FIGURE 4.5. Network analysis of Hollaback!

The network analysis of Hollaback! in Figure 4.5 shows that there is more interaction with the communities from the Global North on anti-rape feminist activism in India. This is an example of how not all anti-rape transnational feminist movements influence, interact, or build public and private agendas in the same way. It is true that, on the whole, feminism is embracing newer paradigms to accommodate both activism and theorizing, owing to social media platforms and the availability of access to the platforms. "The feminist project is becoming increasingly inclusive of many kinds of differences, including among women and across feminist theorizing" (Steiner, 2013, p. 116). However, digital feminist activism operates differently in different countries, sometimes leading to a backlash within the movement and impacting its success.

The Politics of and Backlash against Transnational Feminist Activism

In the previous chapters, the marginalized feminist activists in India and semi-rural journalists admitted that #MeToo or hashtag movements may have had a greater impact in Western countries and in urban areas of India (see interview excerpts in chapter 3). Social media platforms are often portrayed as democratic platforms for marginalized communities and demographics (Chattopadhyay, 2011). In recent years, social media spaces have undergone many changes and updates. Journalists, communication practitioners and scholars have questioned the increasing focus on the social media platforms as catalysts for changes. Gatekeeping within the social media platforms, issues of access, commercialization, and digital literacy are often overlooked (Iosifidis, 2014; Mejias, 2013). I decided to include social media analysis of two of the three rape and murder cases (there were no social media platforms like Facebook and Twitter in 2005 when Pratibha Murthy was raped and murdered). A social media analysis would assess whether social media platforms are truly a democratic space that expresses outrage against rape and pledges support for victims consistently. I question and assess whether social media platforms are as selective as the mainstream media in pledging support for rape victims and trying to build an agenda against rape, irrespective of the social identity of the victim.

Apart from #MeToo, #LoSHA (a list of Indian and Indian-origin academics), a transnational digital feminist movement, started in October 2017 in the Global South by Raya Sarkar, a student of law then based in California. #LoSHA eventually became a successful movement in the Global North (Flaherty, 2018). On November 30, 2017, a crowdsourced survey on sexual harassment in academia in the United States was published by Karen Kelsky, of "The Professor Is In" fame (Flaherty, 2017). A similar list of predatory professors in Indian academia had been published in late October, which resulted in a great deal of backlash from feminist activists such as Nivedita Mennon, Kavita Krishnamurthy, and others in India (Cassin & Prasad, 2017).

Raya Sarkar started and shared a crowdsourced Google Docs file on Facebook listing the names and institutions of professors accused of sexual harassment at universities in India. The list went viral, and it quickly expanded to include complaints against male professors from leading Indian universities. Posted on Facebook, the comments on the post grew. The academics on the list reacted in three different ways through the mainstream media and social media platforms: a handful denied the charges (although some later deleted their posts denying the charges on social media websites), some tried to engage in poetic justice, and others have remained silent. Then the backlash came in the form of an open letter—not from the Right or the accused professors, but from Indian feminists (Anasuya, 2017) who objected that due process had not been followed and pointed to the pitfalls of public naming and shaming.

The debate has been a generational one: the older and well-known feminist activists have accused Raya Sarkar and younger feminist activists of trivializing the feminist movement by indulging in name-calling and sharing names of academics without verifying the allegations. In the letter, the feminist activists say, "This manner of naming can delegitimize the long struggle against sexual harassment and make our task as feminists more difficult" (N. Menon, 2017).

There were rebuttals to these arguments of the feminist activists, including one by Srila Roy, "Whose Feminism Is It Anyway?" (2017), in which she argues that the current disagreement between Indian feminists is not generational but is actually all about caste position—with high-caste women coming down on low-caste women for the way they engage in activism, while fundamentally misunderstanding or overestimating the "legitimate" options they have for fighting sexual harassment.

In later scholarly work (Gajjala, 2019) and other media interviews (Chatterjee, 2018), Raya Sarkar notes that the sexual assault and harassment experiences of women from marginalized communities are still missing and that #MeTooIndia ignored the lower-caste and lower-class women in the movement. Much has been written and discussed regarding class, caste, and religious marginalization in the context of anti-rape and sexual harassment feminist activism and about the role of the media, but the factor of location still largely eludes the discussion (P. Guha, 2017).

One morning in October 2017, I woke up to find the link to this crowdsourced list in an email from my friend Supriya. I scanned it carefully; there were then about sixty names, and the majority of the academics listed belonged to the leading institutions of my birthplace in Kolkata. I couldn't help but see the paradox that the city known for its leftist politics, liberalism, and feminism had the largest number of sex offenders on the list. But why was I surprised? I went to one of the schools listed in the document, and it was a well-established part of campus culture that female students were aware of which professors' offices should never be visited alone, lest he got too close to you. We did not have access to any document, cell phones, or social platforms, but the previous cohorts diligently passed on information by word of mouth. So, what is so different about writing this up in a list? Who exactly is threatened by this act?

#LoSHA also prompted news media coverage in India, but it was very limited in both quality and quantity. The most-circulated English newspapers in India, the *Times of India* and *Hindustan Times*, published only six articles on #LoSHA and #NameAndShame, in which the majority of the articles questioned the intent and focus of the movement (Dasgupta, 2017; Mahapatra, 2017). In the context of naming and shaming perpetrators, one article concludes with the following sentences, effectively questioning the movement: "Will there ever be a campaign to invite the general public to share stories of how some women charmed men to climb the ladders of success? Time will tell" (Mahapatra, 2017).

This limited coverage and gatekeeping by the mainstream media put a question mark on the movement and limited its reach to the public. Gajjala (2018) uses a similar framework to explain this gatekeeping, citing Padmini Ray Murray's work (2017): "Mainstream media reports and characterizations of feminisms in India routinely omit significant Dalit feminist online platforms (such as Savari and Dalit Women Fight) and rural feminist organizations staffed by women from non-dominant caste communities. These presences are often 'only mentioned' [in the media] as an afterthought following a talking head snippet advocating the need for intersectionality" (p. 110).

It all comes down to whose voice is heard in the various media platforms, and whose voice is relegated to the background. In the wake of #MeToo, #LoSHA, and other transnational movements, it has become easier for many to understand that sexual harassment is all about power; wealthy celebrities who control whether a young actress makes it onto the screen, or major news editors who control information to the world have the ability to pressure the women around them. These are exactly the objectively powerful people we think of when we think of high-powered people. However, these patterns play out all over the global economy, across the spectrum of public spaces, academic spaces, and workplaces.

A professor or researcher who has written a few books that circulated only within small academic circles may not seem like a powerful force, but to graduate students and undergraduates who have to gain the attention and interest of these figures in order to have any hope of a lasting career in an uncertain field, these are powerful, gatekeeping celebrities too. Yes, it all comes back to power.

For women who have a position of power at work and in society in general, it is easy enough to say that the public naming and shaming in both #LoSHA and #MeTooIndia is the wrong solution. No doubt there are risks of naming and shaming; after all, it is a classic example of putting words against words with no tangible proof to rely on. This is dangerous territory, and nobody can predict the consequence. Would the list be acceptable if it had another column for the nature of the harassment? Would it help those named recollect how and when they harassed and discriminated against the student? The list itself, however, came about because of a dangerous atmosphere for the least powerful women in academia that has existed for decades. Why aren't these feminists more concerned about the dangers that exist without #thelist or #MeToo?

Due to the gatekeeping in anti-rape and sexual assault activism in India by established activists, sexual violence and assault on women from marginalized communities are often not highlighted in the mainstream media or social media platforms, leading to selective outrage (Dhanaraj, 2018). The truth is that some "establishment" feminist activists in India, many of them academics themselves, are isolated from the realities of daily life for women beneath them. It is true that #thelist and #MeToo are exposing injustices among the relatively elite, restricted to urban higher-education institutions, but this is a start; hopefully, there are more inclusive lists by women who have been harassed by professors in rural and semi-rural areas. Sutapa, who works in rural communities, said, "Many girls who are sexually harassed in rural areas don't speak up because the immediate repercussion would be preventing them from public spaces and academic institutions. What families don't understand is that sexual harassment and assault can happen anywhere, public spaces and private spaces, so the conversation needs to happen around empowering the girls and women. The larger communities in these areas have limited access to social media platforms, other than WhatsApp."

Power plays out in institutions and communities in ways that impact vulnerable women from marginalized communities disproportionately. It is true that social media platforms have given space to discussing issues of sexual abuse or harassment: a Pew research report on the reach of #MeToo on Twitter says that the hashtag has been used more than 19 million times from the date of Alyssa Milano's initial tweet until September 30, 2018 (Anderson & Toor, 2018).

I analyzed textual and nontextual content shared by three feminist activist groups on Facebook in India. The Facebook page of #MeTooIndia was not robust and did not generate any network analysis. The urban and transnational feminist groups, such as Feminism in India and Breakthrough India (see figures 4.6 and 4.7), created strong networks by following Facebook pages of other feminist groups and alternate news websites such as Girls at Dhaba, Upworthy, ScoopWhoop, and others; local feminist and activist groups such as 21st Century India, "Against Rape" (see figure 4.8); mainstream news outlets such as ABP; and political entities such as the Prime Minister's Office, Supporting the Indian Army, and others. Facebook categorizes each page into a pre-assigned group such as community, personality, media organization, news, and others. The feminist groups tend to follow Facebook pages that are classified as community and media organizations.

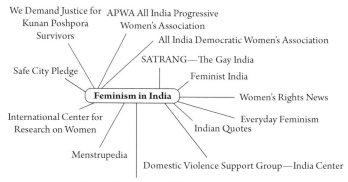

FIGURE 4.6. Network analysis of Feminism in India's Facebook page

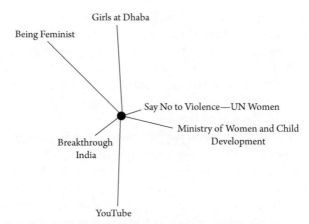

FIGURE 4.7. Network analysis of Breakthrough India's Facebook page

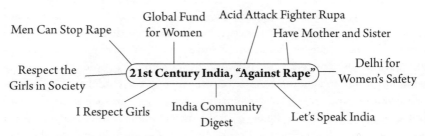

FIGURE 4.8. Network analysis of 21st Century India, "Against Rape"

The feminist activist groups on Facebook posted textual and nontextual content such as images, memes, and videos on equal rights of women, and advocated for judicial action against rape, domestic violence, online trolling, and other related issues. The pages encouraged their followers to comment on their posts and share them. The most shared and commented-on posts were topical. Nontextual content such as images and videos also generated much engagement from the public. The posts were intended for the public and not for policy makers, as most posts asked for the reaction of the people who followed them and also asked them to share their content.

Social Media Analysis of Feminist Pages on Facebook between 2012 and #MeToo

I wanted to analyze the posts and the network connections generated after Jyoti Singh's rape and murder in 2012 and Jisha's rape and murder in 2016. The three pages that I used for this analysis were Breakthrough India, Feminism in India, and 21st Century India, "Against RAPE." I used Gephi as a data visualization tool to create these pages and assessed the categories of page comments, likes, shares and posts, and strongly connected pages in the Facebook network. I completed a detailed analysis of the specific pages and groups in each category. News and media websites were the most popular and the most engaged with on all three webpages.

I analyzed textual and nontextual content shared by three feminist activist groups on Facebook. The feminist groups created strong networks by following Facebook pages of alternate news websites such as Upworthy, ScoopWhoop, and others; feminist and activist groups; and mainstream news outlets such as *ABP, Star News*, the *Times of India*, and others.

Breakthrough India. Breakthrough India is a nonprofit community organization based in New Delhi, India. On its website and Facebook page, Breakthrough India describes itself as "a human rights organization working to make violence and discrimination against women and girls unacceptable." It further explains its work in this way: "Our cutting-edge multimedia campaigns, community mobilization, agenda setting, and leadership training equip men and women worldwide to challenge the status quo and take bold action for the dignity, equality, and justice of all." Created in 2000, Breakthrough India works on various issues, including sexual harassment. I emphasized Breakthrough India's social media campaign in my study, as the organization is known to develop digital and other multimedia campaigns around rape and sexual violence.

The following data visualizations indicate that Breakthrough India was most engaged with the news media and community pages of Facebook. Breakthrough India follows a number of community, media, education, and other categories of pages on Facebook.

In April 2017, Breakthrough India followed 143 pages, with many overlapping categories such as community, causes, nonprofit, and nongovernmental organizations—all of which represent activist groups or pages on Facebook. Similarly, media, news media, news organizations, and publishing all represent groups or pages associated with news and media. To streamline the analysis, I combined the overlapping categories in my calculations. Of the 143 pages that Breakthrough India follows, 94 pages are categorized under community, causes, nonprofit, nongovernmental organizations, and other similar pages related to activism, accounting for 65.7 percent of the total number of pages it follows. Breakthrough India follows 16 pages categorized under media, news media, publication, and magazine, accounting for 11.1 percent of the total number of pages. Finally, government, political leaders, and politics account for 2 percent of the total number of pages. I combined all other categories, such as interest, music, leisure, armed forces, entertainment, and more, in an "other" category since each of these categories had one page under them. The "other" category made up 20.9 percent of the total number of pages. This indicates the tendency of a feminist activism page to connect with other activism-based pages and the media.

I analyzed the strongly connected pages of Breakthrough India's Facebook network in Gephi, an open-source data analysis and data visualization tool. Gephi assessed the strongly connected pages in Breakthrough India's network by abstracting the number of weakly connected components from the number of strongly connected components. The components, or nodes, in a social network that have a strong capability to influence and share information with other components become strongly connected components. The components in a social network that do not have the capability to influence the central component (here the Facebook page) by sharing information become weakly connected. Gephi detected fifty strongly connected nodes or pages and two weakly connected nodes in Breakthrough India's Facebook network. Through Gephi, I was able to identify forty eight strongly connected pages in the network, in which the categories of community or nonprofit and media or news media are the strongly connected nodes. Clinton Global Foundation, Melinda and Bill Gates Foundation, Feminism in India, Hollaback, International Women's Health Network, A Thin Line, Blank Noise, and other similar international organizations make up the strongly connected nodes on this page. Alternate news websites, such as Women's Web and Buzzfeed, are also strongly connected nodes on this page. It is not surprising that Breakthrough India has a strong connection with other international and global nonprofits, as Breakthrough India is an international nonprofit with offices in India and the United States. This helps it create a network with other similar nonprofits or activism groups (see figure 4.7).

Breakthrough India was one of the few organizations that had a Facebook page during Jyoti Singh's rape and murder in 2012 and Jisha's rape and murder in 2016. Breakthrough India created its Facebook page in 2010.

I extracted page and user comments from Breakthrough India's Facebook page for the first two weeks after each rape, following the same pattern I used with the mainstream media. Jyoti Singh was raped on December 16, 2012, and she succumbed to her injuries on December 29, 2012. I wanted to focus on the social media commentary during the first two weeks after Jyoti Singh was raped. I followed the same procedure after Jisha was raped and murdered on April 29, 2016. Table 4.1 notes the quantitative data collected over the two-week period after the rapes and murders of Jyoti and Jisha, respectively.

The numbers indicate that even the digital feminist platforms gave importance to the cases. In digital activism, four years are many light years. Postings over the two-week period increased 1.7 times. In 2016, there were 63 posts over a span of two weeks, 1.7 times more than the same period in 2012, when there were only 37 posts. However, as indicated in table 4.1, despite a lower number of Facebook posts, a higher number of posts were written about Jyoti Singh's rape and murder, as compared with Jisha's rape and murder. Sixty-five percent of the total number of posts focused on Jyoti's rape and murder in 2012, compared with only 41.2 percent of the total posts about Jisha's rape and murder in 2016. In 2012,

Transnational Hashtag Movements

TABLE 4.1. Percentage of comments on Breakthrough India's Facebook page

Name of case	Date range of data collection	Place and date of rape	Total number of comments	Comments on the specific rape	% of total number of comments
Jyoti Singh rape and murder	December 17–31, 2012	Delhi, December 16, 2012	37	25	65
Jisha rape and murder	April 29–May 12, 2016	Peumbavoor, Kerala; April 28, 2016	63	26	41.2

some of the other posts included promotions about a television interview with the vice president of Breakthrough India, gender inequality in the workforce in India, and the campaign against gender violence. In 2016, posts other than those about Jisha's rape and murder included counseling advice for individuals in abusive relationships, open positions for hiring, and solicitations of donations to prevent child marriage and cyberstalking.

Feminism in India. Feminism in India (FII), another leading digital feminist activist group, started its initiative and created a Facebook page in March 2013. The group describes its Facebook page as "an award-winning intersectional feminist digital platform to learn, educate, and develop a feminist sensibility and unravel the F-word among the youth in India. This page aims to raise issues concerning violence and prejudices against women in India as well as other countries. It is a place for debate and discussion and hopes to make people more aware of the current issues."

FII has a network relationship with 127 Facebook pages on communities and nonprofits, media and publishing, government and political leaders, and others (leisure, armed forces, and others). Community, causes, and nonprofits make up 64.5 percent of the total number of pages followed, while media, news media, and publishing is a distant second at 13.8 percent, and government and political leaders are only 6.2 percent. I combined all the other categories because they had only one page categorized under them.

I analyzed the strongly connected pages of FII's Facebook network in Gephi as well. Gephi assessed the strongly connected pages in the FII network by abstracting the number of weakly connected components from the number of strongly connected components. Gephi detected forty-nine strongly connected nodes or pages and one weakly connected node in FII's Facebook network. The strongly connected pages are calculated by subtracting the weakly connected nodes from the strongly connected nodes. Through Gephi, I was able to identify forty eight strongly connected pages in the network, in which the categories of community or nonprofit and media or news media are the strongly connected nodes.

Breakthrough India, SlutWalk Delhi, Blank Noise, Take Back the Tech!, SATRANG—The Gay India, Hollaback, We End Violence, and other similar domestic and international organizations make up the strongly connected nodes on this page. Alternate news websites such as DW: Women Talk Online, Upworthy, and Jaago Re are also strongly connected nodes on this page. FII shares a strong network with similar nonprofits or activism groups and other alternate media pages. It does not share any networks with the mainstream news media.

I also extracted comments posted and shared by FII after Jisha's rape and murder and on the first anniversary of Pandey's rape and murder. In the two weeks after Jisha was raped and murdered, there were a total of ninety-six posts on FII's Facebook page, but only eleven comments discussed Jisha or her rape or murder. FII was initiated in 2013 after Jyoti was raped and murdered in 2012. So, considering the reach and popularity of FII's Facebook page, I analyzed posts published on the first anniversary of Jyoti's rape and murder in 2013. After assessing the Facebook comments after Jyoti Singh's rape and murder, I had expected that engagement with Jisha's rape and murder would be at least 25 percent. Since FII was founded after Jyoti Singh's rape and murder in 2013, I analyzed the posts around the first anniversary of her rape and murder in December of that year. There were a total of 18 percent of the total posts dedicated to Jyoti in Decemebr 2013. In 2016, FII was a more active platform than it was in 2013; when Jisha's rape and murder happened in 2016, I anticipated that there would a higher percentage of posts compared with those about Pandey's rape and murder (see table 4.2).

Even among the top twenty-six comments, which were the most shared, most liked, and most commented-on content, only two comments referred to Jisha. One comment read as follows: "Her name is Jisha. She is NOT Another Nirbhaya. #JusticeForJisha Jisha is a self-made woman. Everything she achieved was through her efforts. Her mother was paranoid who never let anyone near them."

TABLE 4.2. Percentage of the total number of comments on Feminism in India Facebook page

Name of case	Date range of data collection	Place and date of rape	Total number of comments	Comments on the specific rape	% of total number of comments
Jyoti Singh rape and murder	December 16–31, 2013	Delhi, December 16, 2012	32	6	18.75
Jisha rape and murder	April 29–May 12, 2016	Peumbavoor, Kerala; April 28, 2016	96	11	11.46

The next post was more detailed, exploring the caste and class intersectionality of Jisha, and pinpointing how mainstream media reports on sexual violence against Dalit women:

Been reading a lot of articles written in the aftermath of Jisha's rape and murder asking is Kerala really safe for women? or is Kerala STILL safe for women? So please let me break it to you: Kerala isn't safe for women. It never has been safe for women. And it never will be safe for women. It is patriarchal and it is casteist. And no 100% literacy doesn't make a shit of a difference. Kerala is home for me—I have a number of fond memories of spending weeks at my grandmother's house learning how to make flower garlands listening to endless stories of *Mahabharata* and *Ramayana* arguing with her about whether God really exists. But it's also peppered with some of my worst memories of harassment—being groped, flashed, stalked, and leered at by men on the streets in broad daylight. All this despite making it a point to dress in the baggiest of clothes, seem as inconspicuous as possible, and never stepping out alone after 6 P.M. We seem to have woken up to gender violence in Kerala only after the brutal rape and murder of Dalit law student Jisha (we all know her name because the media didn't find her caste and class status worthy enough to be given some patronizing title like Amanat or Damini: except of course some scattered references to her as Kerala's Nirbhaya). Her mother has stated that she was in constant fear for Jisha's security, so much that she had given her daughter a pen camera—because neighbors had been threatening her constantly and she was regularly subjected to street harassment. They complained to the cops who did nothing because didn't you know as a woman street harassment comes as a part and parcel of daily life? So again we waited till she was raped murdered left to die with her intestines hanging out of her body till we could give a shit (that too only days after the actual incident because nobody really cared to report on it till then—after all, she's a Dalit does it really make a difference to our privileged and casteless lives?) I've said it before and I'm saying it again: violence against a woman isn't only real when it's rape. It's real when she is groped on the street; it's real when a man tries to touch himself sitting next to her on a bus, it's real when she's whistled at and called baby or pataka. Let's maybe start giving a shit about women while they are alive instead of waiting for them to die and turning them into martyrs. I'm sure her name has been revealed because of some other reasons and not because she was a Dalit. A human being is a human being; adding a caste like Dalit or SC doesn't change anything.

On its Facebook page, FII similarly followed and engaged with media organizations such as ScoopWhoop, Upworthy, Youth Ki Awaaz, and others. FII follows alternative sources of media. Most of these are not mainstream media organizations but alternative news websites, which are only available online.

80   HEAR #METOO IN INDIA

After Jisha's rape and murder, the posts published on FII's Facebook page focused on the location, caste identity of Jisha as a Dalit, and Nirbhaya (Jyoti Singh). I see this as Jisha's identity being overlooked and Nirbhaya's identity overriding Jisha's. Jisha has a separate identity, so giving her the title of "Kerala's Nirbhaya" or "Nirbhaya 2" is taking her identity away, because Jisha's social identity is different from that of Jyoti Singh (Nirbhaya). Jisha was a Dalit, and Jyoti Singh was an upper-caste woman. Jisha was from the southern state of Kerala, and Jyoti Singh was from the country's capital, New Delhi. These are significant differences in discussing the social identity of the victim.

21st Century India, "Against Rape." 21st Century India, "Against Rape" is another digital advocacy group that created a Facebook page in December 2012. It initiated its activism in December 2012, after Jyoti Singh's rape and murder. Its Facebook page describes its agenda as follows: "Raise Your Voice against RAPE AND ACID ATTACKS. Developed Platform to Raise Voice Against RAPE AND ACID ATTACKS." This is one of the most active pages on Facebook on anti-rape activism in India.

21st Century India, "Against Rape" has a network relationship with 114 Facebook pages on communities and nonprofits, media and publishing, government and political leaders, and others (leisure, armed forces, and others).

I used the visualization software Gephi to understand the connections between the strongly connected social network of 21st century India, "Against Rape" on Facebook. Gephi identified the top-most connect nodes, that have a strong capability to influence and share information between them become strongly connected components. The components or nodes in a social network that do not have the ability to influence the central component (read Facebook page) by sharing information become weakly connected components. Gephi calculated that there were 102 strongly connected components in the network and 1 weakly connected component, which resulted in 101 strongly connected components in the Facebook network of the page. Community or nonprofit and media or news media were the strongly connected nodes on this page. CARMA, TrustBetrayed-JusticeDemanded, PriceOfSilence SaathBeingTogether, and other similar domestic organizations make up the strongly connected nodes on this page. Unlike the previous pages, this page has strong connections with mainstream media pages on Facebook such as Channel 4 News, *Navbharat Times*, and others, which are also strongly connected nodes on this page. 21st Century India, "Against Rape" is connected with many domestic and rural nonprofit groups on Facebook, unlike Breakthrough India, which has strong connections with international nonprofits.

I extracted comments from this page after the rapes and murders of Pandey and Jisha. Unsurprisingly, this group also focused on Pandey's rape and murder more than Jisha's, which is evident from the number of posts shared on Face-

Transnational Hashtag Movements

TABLE 4.3. Percentage of comments on the Facebook page of 21st century India, "Against Rape"

Name of case	Date range of data collection	Place and date of rape	Total number of comments	Comments on the specific rape	% of the total number of comments
Jyoti Singh rape and murder	December 17–31, 2012	Delhi, December 16, 2012	17	16	94.11
Jisha rape and murder	April 29–May 12, 2016	Peumbavoor, Kerala; April 28, 2016	3	20	15

book. Table 4.3 gives an overview of the engagement of this Facebook page with the specific incidents.

The type of comments also differed between the cases. After Pandey's rape, most comments from followers, and the owner of the page, discussed the type of punishment that the rapists deserved. There were detailed discussions on the quantum of punishment that rapists should be given. One of the top comments, which was the most shared, engaged with, and liked, was the demand for the castration of the rapists.

21st Century India, "Against Rape" framed women not as individuals but as daughters, mothers, wives, and honored possessions of the country. Their worth is defined by the gendered role they play in their families.

Dependence on the News Media

I decided to compare the media coverage of the rapes and murders of Pratibha Murthy, Jyoti Singh, and Jisha and the rape of the Unnao victim for the following reasons:

1. The rapes and murders provided a timeline for me to identify changes in the reporting of rape incidents after social media platforms became ubiquitous in newsrooms and publication communication.
2. The 2012 gang-rape incident is often referred to as a watershed moment in feminist activism in India by scholars and journalists. I wanted to analyze the response to the 2016 rape case and understand whether there had been a change in rape coverage or whether the coverage of the 2012 gang-rape case was an outlier. There were many similarities between the 2012 and the 2016 gang-rape cases, but a comparison of mainstream media coverage would indicate whether the framing of rape and sexual assault had really changed and whether it was consistent in similarly brutal incidents.

3. The Unnao rape victim's near-death experience happened after the #MeToo movement gained momentum. Therefore, it is imperative to analyze the impact of the news media on the coverage of her rape and attack.

Journalists in India are required to follow certain laws when they report on rape and sexual assault. During the interviews, many journalists pointed out that despite their best intentions not to victimize rape survivors, the Indian legal structure and laws complicate the coverage of rape. The complications arise from the misunderstandings of the journalists regarding when and how they should identify the victims. Even when the victims or their families are willing to identify themselves, the newsrooms refrain from recognizing the victims.

Journalists steadfastly follow the Indian Penal Code when they are reporting on rape and sexual assault. According to the Central Government Act, Section 228A, of the Indian Penal Code, disclosing the identity of the victim in any publication is punishable by imprisonment and monetary fine (Zeldin, 2013). However, if the victim or, upon the death of the victim, the next of kin gives a written statement to the officer in charge agreeing to be identified by the media, the news outlets may identify the victim. Some of the interview participants, such as journalists Subhro and Amit, agreed that anonymity leads to further victimization of the individual. Although they appreciate the logic behind the law—that is, to protect the rape victim from being harassed—it prevents journalists from disclosing important facts in their news reports, such as whether the victim was stalked by a neighbor or whether the victim had previously filed a complaint in a local police precinct. These discussions would not be possible without identifying the victim in some way, such as the neighborhood in which she lived. It also conveniently dehumanizes the victim if there is no name.

I discuss this issue up front because of the inconsistency in disclosing the identities of the victims in the three rape cases in the study. Pratibha Murthy Srikanth and Jisha were identified by the press, and their images were circulated through the media. I do not know if Pratibha Murthy Srikanth's family gave permission to the media to identify her in media reports. Jisha's last name is unknown; in the media coverage, she was identified as Jisha. However, I do know that, in Jyoti Singh's coverage, she was not identified by the press until her parents came forward to disclose her identity, and her image has also not been made public on any media platform thus far. Similarly, the Unnao rape victim's identity has never been made public. In contrast, Jisha was not given any alias by the media; her real name and image were widely circulated by the media. There could be two reasons for this:

1. Jisha, a *Dalit* woman, is at the bottom of the caste hierarchy; hence, she is not given the same courtesy as upper-caste victims (Basu, 2016).

2. Initially, it was believed by the police that Jisha was murdered and assaulted and not raped. In such cases, the law to withhold identity is not applicable (Mantri, 2016).

The inconsistency in the coverage of the rapes and the erratic quantity and quality of coverage given to the cases negatively impact the agenda-building process.

Background

Pratibha Murthy, a twenty-eight-year-old married woman working at the business processing office (BPO) of Hewlett Packard in Bangalore, India, was raped and murdered on December 24, 2005, in Bangalore, by her driver. Murthy belonged to an upper-middle-class family. Murthy's rape and murder prompted media discussions about the safety of working women in big cities, the change in work culture due to the IT boom in India, and the responsibility of multinational companies in ensuring the safety of their employees. According to news reports and police investigations, Murthy and another female employee of the organization had previously complained about the driver's harassment and misbehavior, but the company, which had contract drivers on its roster, did not act to remove him from duty. Although another driver was scheduled to pick her up on December 24, the information did not reach Murthy. She was reported missing after she left home for her night shift. When she did not turn up at her workplace, a missing person report was filed; a few days later, her body was recovered. Police investigations concluded that she had been raped and murdered. The newspaper coverage emphasized Murthy's family and background and the safety of the call centers (Hegde, 2011).[1] The rape and murder soon became more than a crime against Murthy; the rape became a crime against her family, as the family had lost not only a member but also their honor (Hegde, 2011; "BPO Employee," 2010). After Murthy's rape and murder, the government forced the multinational organizations and call centers to overhaul organizational policies regarding the safety and security of women (Nandi, 2012).

Jyoti Singh was gang-raped and murdered on December 16, 2012, in Delhi. This case, in which a young paramedic student was gang-raped and brutalized by four men on a bus, is often referred to as a watershed moment in feminist activism. Pandey had gone to watch a movie with a male friend, Awindra Pandey (no relation). After the movie, Jyoti and her friend were not able to arrange suitable public transport. "They took a rickshaw but the driver refused to take them the full distance and dropped them in the middle of nowhere" (Bukhari, 2013). While Jyoti and Awindra were waiting on an isolated road, an empty white bus stopped in front of them and the driver asked where they were headed to. Once they got on, they realized that they were the only passengers. After fifteen to twenty minutes of riding, the three driver's assistants started harassing Jyoti and her friend. It started as a verbal attack and harassment but quickly escalated to threats and sexual harassment. When Jyoti and her friend protested, they were severely beaten. Jyoti was then raped by the assistants and the driver while the other assistants took turns driving the bus. Jyoti put up a fight against her perpetrators; in retaliation, one of them shoved a rod through her vagina.

Around 9 P.M., Jyoti and her friend were thrown from the moving bus onto a secluded road. Some people passing by noticed them and took them to the hospital. There were brief media reports on Jyoti's rape the following day. As more information came to light, protests grew across the country. Per Indian law, the media cannot identify a rape victim, so some Indian news publications changed the name of the victim. One publication called Jyoti "Nirbhaya," which means "the fearless." Another publication gave her the name Damini, which is the name of a famous movie character from the 1990s who fought for the rights of a rape and murder victim. Nirbhaya became the more famous pseudonym, though her parents repeatedly said they were not ashamed to identify their daughter with her name. There were widespread protests in Delhi, where the crime took place, and in multiple places across the country. During the protests, chaos broke out between the police and the protesters. As Jyoti's condition worsened, she was moved from Delhi to Singapore for her medical treatment by the government. Journalists followed her and her family to Singapore. On December 29, Pandey succumbed to her injuries. However, before dying, she identified her perpetrators and gave a detailed statement to the police on the incident and how she was raped and violently assaulted.[2] This created a huge movement and a spike in social media engagement (Ahmed, Jaidka, & Cho, 2017).

NDTV (2012) published the following on its website after the death of Jyoti: "The Nirbhaya case had drawn a visceral response from the nation. Protests and candlelight marches held across all metros. The biggest of these were held in Delhi, where thousands of students braved tear gas shells and water cannons at the India Gate in bitter winter."

The death of Jyoti Singh resulted in worldwide protests and uproar. Protests against Pandey's rape and murder spilled over onto social media sites, and #Nirbhaya was a top trending hashtag on Twitter (Biswas, 2016). Numerous Facebook pages were created on the theme of justice for Nirbhaya, demanding safety for women on public transport, safety in public spaces, and castration of rapists. Meanwhile, the perpetrators were arrested and taken into police custody. Academics (Belair-Gagnon, Mishra, & Agur, 2014; Durham, 2015; Rao, 2014) and journalists have repeatedly emphasized the narrative that social media platforms made a huge difference in making this a watershed moment in rape coverage and social justice. As an outcome, the government proposed to establish rape crisis centers and constituted the Justice Verma Commission. The PRS Legislative report describes the Justice Verma Commission as follows: "A three-member committee headed by Justice J. S. Verma, former Chief Justice of the Supreme Court, was constituted to recommend amendments to the Criminal Law so as to provide for quicker trial and enhanced punishment for criminals accused of committing sexual assault against women. The other members on the committee were Justice Leila Seth, former judge of the High Court, and Gopal Subramanium, former Solicitor General of India" ("Complaints of Sexual Harrassment," 2019).

The committee submitted its report on January 23, 2013. It made recommendations on laws related to rape, sexual harassment, trafficking, child sexual abuse, and medical examination of victims, as discussed in chapter 1.

In the third case, Jisha,[3] a thirty-year-old Dalit law student, was raped and murdered in Kerala by her stalker on April 28, 2016, in Perumbavoor (Kerala). In both the mainstream media and social media, parallels were quickly drawn to the rape and murder of Jyoti Singh. The media coverage discussed in depth the gory details of Jisha's murder (such as that she was stabbed over thirty times and her intestines were removed). The initial narrative resembled the coverage of Jyoti's rape and murder, but the outrage in Jisha's rape and murder was significantly less than that of Jyoti's rape and murder. There were no candlelight vigils and no swift action against the perpetrator. Within a few weeks, the conversation and engagement fizzled. The Twitter hashtag was present for only a couple of days. Here, a lower-caste (Dalit) woman was brutally raped and murdered, but there was less mass outrage against Jisha's rape and murder. Geetika Mantri, in her May 4, 2016, article in *The News Minute*, noted that some media coverage indicated that the brutality in this case was greater than that of the Delhi gang-rape case, but it failed to get similar attention from the media or policy makers.

In the three cases, media practitioners and scholars have widely accepted that Jyoti Singh's rape and murder is considered a watershed moment because of the changes in rape and sexual harassment laws in India, much like the 1970 Mathura rape case.[4] Changes were made in Indian rape law on the recommendation of the Justice Verma Commission, such as allowing the victims to file an online First Information Report (FIR), setting up rape crisis centers, ensuring that the police help the victims irrespective of their jurisdiction, and more. The central government created the Criminal Law (Amendment Act) of 2013 to make sexual assaults and rape laws robust and sensitive to the victim. Section 53A of the Indian Evidence Act was modified, which made the previous sexual experiences and relationships of the victim in a case of sexual assault and rape irrelevant when establishing consent. The 2013 law also prohibited questioning the victim regarding past sexual relations and experiences during witness examination in court. In May 2013, the Supreme Court of India banned the two-finger test, also known as the virginity test, for a rape victim, citing that it violates the privacy of the victims. The two-finger test was conducted on rape survivors by inserting two fingers into the woman's vagina to check her virginity. All these changes came into the legal system after the rape and murder of Jyoti Singh Pandey. There have been many incidents of rape and murder after Jyoti Singh's, but none have garnered similar public outrage or media sympathy.

In 2018, a seventeen-year-old minor girl from rural Uttar Pradesh, Unnao, was raped and assaulted by the local political leader ("Unnao Rape Victim," 2018). However, the survivor received negligible support from the administration, including disinterest from the police in filing her case. She received death threats, her father died in police custody, and she tried to immolate herself in front of the chief minister's house. In April 2018, there were some public protests for her along with the protests for Asifa, the eight-year-old rape victim at Kathua ("Kathua Rape Case," 2018). However, the rape survivor from Unnao and her ordeal were quickly relegated to the background after the government handed the case over to the Central Bureau of Investigation and the accused political leader from the ruling party in the state was arrested. For more than a year, there was neither any follow-up coverage in the news media nor any social media hashtags for the rape survivor from Unnao. In July 2019, when the Unnao survivor was traveling with her family and lawyer for a hearing, their car was involved in an accident that killed her family members and left her and her lawyer in critical condition ("Unnao Rape Survivor Critical," 2019). Media reports alleged that the accident was an attempt to kill the survivor ("Unnao Rape Survivor Critical," 2019), leading to the Supreme Court's intervention to complete the investigation and the expulsion of the accused from the political party. Around this time, there were also limited hashtag outrages on social media platforms such as Twitter demanding justice for the Unnao survivor. When a news portal interviewed the injured mother of the Unnao rape survivor a few days after the accident, she said that the news media had deserted them six months ago. "Only you (the media) can give us justice. I have been talking to the media constantly since this *hadsaa* (incident) happened, but six months ago, the media was nowhere to be seen. If you desert us, how can we expect justice?" (Dutt, 2019). This categorically points out the dependence on the news media for agenda building and justice in rural India. At the end of the interview, the survivor's mother reiterates that only the media can help them get through the difficult times: "'I hope she gets well. *Pata nahin*, I don't know, I hope it's nothing serious. Please pray that she recovers. Only you (the media) can help us through this,' she says, her voice quivering for the first time" (Dutt, 2019).

The Unnao rape survivor, much like the Suryanelli rape survivor, did not become a Nirbhaya or an Asifa for the country. There were a few candlelight vigils but no social media uproar or hashtag movements, and no culmination in a larger digital movement. At the time of writing this book, the Unnao rape victim is still in critical condition and on life support, fighting for her life (Rashid, 2019).

In 2018, an online news portal interviewed the Unnao rape survivor when #MeToo and #MeTooIndia were raging on social media sites; unsurprisingly, she was not aware of the movement and did not know that it had forced a central government minister from the same party to resign (Dhingra, 2018).

To Dhingra (2018), she said, "I don't have a phone, I don't watch TV, so I have no idea what is going on. . . . The only thing that is on my mind is my father," she said. "Had I kept quiet about what happened with me, he would have been with us. . . . I keep thinking about him all day. What has speaking up given me? The government has done nothing for me or my family—no aid, no compensation. . . . I have just lost my father."

There is no doubt that the Unnao rape survivor was failed by both the news media and social media in consistent coverage and conversation about her rape and assault. The lack of digital access not only makes rural and marginalized women vulnerable to rape and sexual assault, when no one speaks for them, but also supports the system in harassing them, which they cannot share online.

Politicization of Rape. The rape of the minor girl in Unnao was highly politicized, as the perpetrator was a legislative member of the current ruling party. Not only did the perpetrator wield power and influence over the victim, but the fact that the rape happened in rural northern India also did not generate any media coverage or public outcry. As one of the interviewees lamented, "The public and media reaction to the rural rapes are very predictable, such things happen and our readers are not interested in knowing more about it." Chinmaya agreed that the victim had a harrowing time even filing a case against the perpetrator because of the system and the apathy of the police officers. The fact that the rape happened in 2017 and the victim has been fighting for justice since then, coinciding with the #MeToo and #MeTooIndia movement online, did not lead to support or help for her in any way. One would think that the #MeToo and #MeTooIndia movements would help ensure justice in such a high-visibility case, but alas, this did not happen.

Rural Rape Not in Focus. Repeatedly, journalists, editors, and rural feminist activists have focused on the fact that rural or semi-rural rape is not the focus of the mainstream news media in India. Unfortunately, rural or semi-rural rape is not even the focus of social media activism. Since it is not within the purview of either news or social media, it often falls into the gap between them. Sometimes, the rural and semi-rural activists do not have access to digital media platforms, and when they do, they often lack digital literacy and have a hard time going through the workings of them. The fact that they are not connected with the larger public sphere through Facebook, Twitter, WhatsApp, and Instagram keeps their struggles limited.

The mainstream news media also does not feel the pressure to publish on rural or semi-rural rapes because they are not pressured by social media or candlelight marches on the streets. Most of the time, the episodic framing of rape and sexual assault, especially those involving a politician in rural and semi-rural India, casts it as a scandal and does not go into the deeper issues of discrimination and lack of support from the government and law agencies. No one wants to support their struggles, other than a few candlelight marches. There are waves of support— only when something drastic happens.

Bollywoodization. Bollywood or the film industry and fraternity has been in the eye of the storm of the #MeTooIndia movement since multiple women actors, directors, and other professionals accused male Bollywood professionals of sexual harassment, rape, and assault. However, the outcome was a disappointment as either most of the accused were acquitted or no cases were registered against them, and they continued to work confidently in the industry. It is ironic that the same Bollywood industry uses social media platforms for anti-rape and sexual harassment activism. This usually has multiple issues; the Bollywood professionals often tie in a campaign with an upcoming film and use it to stay in the news cycle. That they engage in selective outrage calls their integrity into question. Finally, they lack consistency, which is repeatedly questioned in the media.

Overshadowed by Other Rapes. The Unnao rape happened in 2017, but it was not until 2018 that there were any displays of activism or candlelight marches. In April 2018, Asifa, an eight-year-old girl, was gang-raped and murdered on religious premises in Jammu and Kashmir. There was a public movement against Asifa's rape and murder, including candlelight marches in cities and social media activism involving turning one's profile picture black. There were WhatsApp messages, Twitter hashtags, and Facebook posts to bring the perpetrators to justice. This was around the same time that the rape of the Unnao victim became public, more than a year after it happened. She tried to commit suicide in front of the state chief minister's house after her father was falsely implicated and died in police custody ("Unnao Rape Victim," 2018). Until then, there was no demand for justice for the Unnao victim.

The Asifa and Unnao rapes together became the focus of a public movement involving both social media platforms and the news media, motivating the authorities to take further action in the cases. Every now and then there would be a follow-up on Asifa's case in the news media and social media, and her perpetrators were eventually punished in 2019. However, the Unnao rape victim and her plight quickly slipped from the memories of the public and the media. Rape and sexual assaults become news and social media campaigns when they are outliers due to their heinous and shocking nature. The Unnao rape victim was alive, alone, and staying in a rural area; unfortunate as it may sound, neither the public nor the media took up her cause, "as such things happen in villages" (Rashid, 2019).

It took a vehicle accident leading to the deaths of a victim's family members and her own near-death condition to motivate the public and the media to write about the injustices and negligence of law enforcement. Eventually, after many years, the police arrested the perpetrator to take the case forward.

Leading to Suicide by Police Inaction. Between 2013 and 2015, the number of rape and sexual harassment cases registered at precinct in India had increased exponentially. In rural and semi-rural areas, going to the police station (precinct) involves facing indignities, especially for rural and lower-caste women. An urban activist who works closely with a rural activist said, on the condition of anonymity, "When she goes to the precinct to help the victims of sexual assault file simple FIR, they are mocked because of their caste. She has to keep persisting before they take their complaint. A lot of times, she is hounded by the perpetrators and she has to go into hiding. How do we expect social media to work in such cases?" In September 2019, a woman in a semi-rural area committed suicide outside the police station because of police inaction in her case (PTI, 2019). This was reported in a newspaper, but there was no active campaign (PTI, 2019). Rapes and sexual assaults like these remind us that social media campaigns against rape and sexual assault are a good start but not inclusive and leave a gap for marginalized communities. Perhaps that is one of the reasons that the news media in such situations still have an impact.

Datafication of the Movement. Anti-rape and sexual assault feminist activism are not new; they have been a part of the larger feminist movement, workplace harassment conversation, and political policies since the 1970s (the second wave of the feminist movement). However, the hashtag movement has made it possible for these conversations to be tracked and measured. A study conducted by PERIO (GWU) highlights the virality of the #MeToo movement: "When you compare the #MeToo 'moment' to other sexual harassment conversations on Twitter since 2010, #MeToo stands out as uniquely viral by both measures" (Ohlheiser, 2018). This is similar to the Bollywoodization of anti-rape feminist activism in India, where celebrities have helped draw the attention of the media to the issue by sharing their experiences of sexual assault and harassment. However, this also has the tendency to fizzle out once celebrities are no longer a part of the conversation, which is a dangerous precedent as the movement takes it as selective outrage, undermining the movement and the grassroots activists, who have limited resources and media exposure. Yes, social media sites such as Twitter and Facebook do give a voice to marginalized communities, but access and social media literacy are a big question that is often overlooked in anti-rape feminist activism. The issues of datafication also overlook the issues of contextualization and limitations of data. Virality and datafication have the issue of oversimplifying the movement and making a movement grand in comparison with its impact on the ground. Datafication of the movement also does not treat the scale and virality of the movement globally. Some First World countries with less of a digital divide and more access have unequal online representation compared with others. This has the issue of overshadowing the grassroots activists and hijacking their cause.

Rape Culture and the Press. In recent years, researchers and journalists have identified the existing rape culture in the press—that is, how rape is framed in mainstream mass media, expressing sympathy with the rapists and questioning the victims, all of which is not new but it still exists. It is possible to bring out these facts and focus on them when the language of reporting is English, but what happens when local languages are involved? Most rural audiences in India are undoubtedly less reported on in mainstream English media. The rural language press is also understudied, so it is difficult to assess the victim blaming. The rural audience has access to this kind of press.

One Year Later. It is not surprising to see that a year after #MeTooIndia started its second phase in 2018, there has been limited discussion of its successes and failures. The legal implications associated with the movement have pushed back some of the encouraging narratives. The online tweets and Facebook comments are encouraging for younger girls in rural areas to understand that a movement is taking place, but they are not enough for them to feel emboldened to speak up. One of the reasons for holding back is limited support from the community and their families. Going public could result in repercussions, including curtailing basic freedoms and education. It is never easy to go public, even after many years, as the perpetrators may be in the vicinity, and going public could impact the victims/survivors. The hierarchization of the #MeToo movement has affected who is included and who is not. Moving away from established feminists has also created issues of credibility in the movement. These issues were in the news in 2019 when most of the perpetrators were normalizing their way back into public life.

A year on, oppositional movements such as #HimToo have started in the social media realms against alleged false allegations of rape and sexual harassment by women against men ("Govt Dissolves #MeToo Panel Quietly," 2019). A few new media articles argued that #MeToo could become a witch hunt, thus giving rise to the #HimToo movement ("After What Has Happened," 2019).

Normalizing the Trend. In 2019, Harvey Weinstein was seen in a public space enjoying the performances of young women comedians. He was invited by the organizers. Similarly, Anu Malik, accused of sexual harassment during #MeTooIndia in 2018, was invited back as a judge on a reality television show in 2019. M. J. Akbar, a former minister of state for external affairs accused by several women in the newsroom, was back in public life, and no case was registered against Nana Patekar because the witnesses refused to speak.

As much as the hashtag movements on sexual harassment open up space for women and other marginalized individuals to share their experiences and seek justice, the movements also have an issue of sustainability after visibility. Most hashtag movements tend to fizzle out after the initial successful visibility, resulting in normalizing the issue of sexual harassment and abuse at the workplace. The

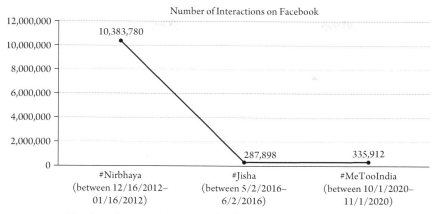

FIGURE 4.9. Number of interactions on Facebook, originating from India on #Nirbhaya, #Jisha, #MeTooIndia. From Facebook CrowdTangle data.

accused are back in the workplace, and the activists have a difficult time keeping the agenda in line. After the candlelight vigils in India against sexual violence and rape, there were no follow-ups. The social media platforms move quickly from one issue to another. Bots on social media do not make it easier for activism concerning any issues of sexual harassment, as they have the capacity to make any topic or issue the trend; many times, sexual harassment and rape fall into the gaps. See figure 4.9 for the number of Facebook interactions that happen on #MetooIndia. It is many fewer than #Nirbhaya, and comparable with #Jisha, in the first month that it started. Discourses on social media platforms and the ability to make it successful depends on the intensity, volume, and reach of the interactions.

The Role of Mainstream Media. At a time when the mainstream media is often termed as biased and "fake," the social media platforms provide an alternate space for views and news. However, dependence on any particular media platform alone, whether it be a mass media or social media platform, has its own pitfalls. None of the media platforms is foolproof. So far as activism is concerned in a diverse country like India, social media and the news media are not interchangeable. The most recent circulation numbers of newspapers in India are impressive and go against the general downward trend. Newspaper circulation is still going up, including for regional language newspapers. Surprisingly, the Unnao rape did not find many takers in the regional language newspapers. The Unnao rape victim has been discharged from the hospital, but there has not been much to report on.

The Role of Affinity Groups on Facebook. Social media creates affinity groups for women, connecting them on various issues. However, most of the affinity groups do not deal with sexual harassment or rape. They mostly discuss domestic violence and other things that are socially acceptable as topics. The groups that are related to activism discuss various things beyond rape and sexual assault. The only group to focus exclusively on rape and sexual assault is in an Indian language—moving beyond the English-speaking urban population. Unfortunately, we will need to wait until the next time a heinous rape takes place before we see another social media and mass media uproar. Until then, everyday sexual harassment is, unfortunately, regularized.

During the thematic analysis of the news coverage of the three rapes in this project, I remembered the thoughtful words of one of the interviewees on sexual abuse and harassment in marginalized communities and the lack of media support for them: "How will the girls fight back when sexual harassment and abuse is part of their daily lives? How do they share their experiences online even when they have access?" As someone who is very guarded in sharing personal experiences on social media platforms, I understand the predicament of the girls and women in sharing their experiences. The freedom they receive from social media platforms will be gone. This predicament makes them vulnerable. The grassroots-level activists are often not sure if social media platforms amplify their voices enough to be able to reach the policy makers. They are aware that, as the fourth estate, the news media reaches the policy makers and has the capacity to influence policy making. Awareness of social media platforms on sexual harassment is not the issue; rather, it is understanding its impact on policy making and, in turn, on the lives of these girls and women.

Journalism and communication are evolutionary due to the changes in the platforms. Journalism and communication platforms should ideally connect advocacy with policy makers, including on the issues of rape and sexual assault. Rape and sexual assault are no longer taboo topics.

As I discussed earlier, location has always been an important factor in building an anti-rape and sexual assault agenda in India. The Unnao rape and attempted murder happened to a rural-based victim; thus, for the urban Twitterati and news media, this rape was off their radar for sustained reporting and activism. Table 4.4 shows the themes in the news coverage of the four rapes that was published in the two most widely circulated English-language newspapers two weeks after the rapes and murders happened. For the Unnao rape victim, I have included the news articles from 2018, for the first two weeks after she and her family faced violence from the perpetrator. She was raped in 2017, but none of the English newspapers carried that report, despite the involvement of a high-profile political leader in her rape.

In this study, I only went back to 2005 to compare coverage of rape in Indian English-language media in recent years. The preliminary findings across the themes indicate that there have been a few changes in rape coverage. In Table 4.4, I have listed the number of times each theme occurred in the coverage of the rapes and murders of Murthy, Pandey, and Jisha, with the Unnao rape victim's

TABLE 4.4. Themes in the news coverage of the four rapes

Theme	Pratibha Murthy's rape and murder coverage	Jyoti Singh's rape and murder coverage	Jisha's rape and murder coverage	Unnao rape victim's coverage 166 articles TOI = 84 and HT = 82
News value	0	383	21	0
Location	3	227	127	10
Caste and class	2	235	39	95
Politicizing rape	12	279	25	166
Public agenda	2	101	33	32
Mentions on social media platforms	N/A	Facebook: 119 Twitter: 65 Social media: 28 Total: 212	Facebook: 2 Twitter: 0 Social media: 8 Total: 10	N/A
Mentions by activists	2	123	4	12
Victim blaming	0	2	4	5

KEY: HT = *Hindustan Times*; TOI = *The Times of India*

news coverage. Compared with the media coverage of the rapes and murders of Murthy and Jisha and of the sexual violence of the Unnao rape victim, Jyoti's rape coverage was significantly more extensive. It would not be a stretch to state that the coverage and attention given to Jyoti's rape and murder was an outlier. Overall, there was an increase in references to sound bites from celebrities, promoting the newspaper agenda, references to the public agenda, references to caste and class, and the geographical location of the victim. Some of the themes in rape and sexual assault coverage have seen few changes, like references to activists and the kind of work they are involved in to spread awareness against rape and sexual assault. There is a clear gap between the coverage of rape and sexual assault and the work done by activists and activist groups to combat rape and sexual assault. In the recent past—specifically, after social media platforms became popular and accessible to the public—there has been an increase in the references to public opinion and identifying the public agenda in cases of rape and sexual assault.

However, rape and sexual assault of similar brutality still get inconsistent and uneven coverage. Victims of rape and sexual assault are valued according to their social and geographical identities, which is evident in the news coverage.

Rape continues to be a political issue—whenever rape and sexual assault happens during election campaigns, it becomes an issue related to the campaign, party, and candidate. In such cases, the media framing and focus is often not on the failure of the policy but on the "political scandal" of the incident. This results in politicizing the coverage of rape and gives prominence to the political leaders and political issues, distracting attention from addressing the issues and reasons that lead to rape and sexual assault.

The media coverage of the rapes and murders of both Murthy and Pandey led to policy changes. Business process outsourcing (BPO), information technology (IT) and information technology–enabled services (ITES), industries in which women worked late-night shifts, were now required to provide security for women who were the last passengers in their carpools to be dropped off. Usually, male colleagues would offer to be dropped off last. As a journalist in India, I have done many night shifts at work, and I was often the first or second one dropped off in my carpool. The only time I was dropped off last was when the carpool had six women returning home at 2 A.M. in a flooded city. After Pandey's rape and murder, the Verma commission was instituted, and the recommendations included an overhaul of policies for rape and sexual assault victims, which resulted in the Criminal Law Amendment Act of 2013. The media covered the recommendations widely. However, from Jisha's rape and murder, it can be assumed that not much had changed on the ground. After Jisha was raped and murdered, her mother and sister alleged that Jisha was stalked and harassed and that law enforcement did not register her case. Her complaint was dismissed as verbal abuse, and no complaint was registered. The mainstream media did not cover these details, but alternative news websites such as Quartz and a few other news blogs discovered this. This happened despite the fact that Jisha's rape and murder were politicized during the election campaign, but there were no concrete outcomes such as providing training to law enforcement or integrating the work of anti-rape activists to spread awareness on rape and sexual assault. The social and geographical identities of the victims and the perpetrators have been a consistent pattern in rape and sexual assault coverage. Higher-caste rape and sexual assault victims are explicitly indicated by the repeated use of their last names. In contrast, when the victim is of a lower caste, this is clearly stated in the news coverage. The emphasis on the caste affiliation of the victims has remained consistent, irrespective of the influence of social media platforms in newsroom rape coverage. Many have accused mainstream media of withholding information due to corporate, political compulsion, or social biases (Jolly, 2016; Fadnis, 2017). This gatekeeping also contributes to the consistent patterns in rape and sexual assault coverage.

GAPS BETWEEN MEDIA PLATFORMS

Past studies have shown that the media sets an agenda for the public (McCombs, 2014). In recent studies, there has been a focus on the agenda-building capacity of new media platforms such as Facebook, Twitter, and blogs (Messner & Garrison, 2010). Media platforms have different audiences, and depending on the audience, the platforms present and focus on the news in different ways (Schrøder, 2015). Often media platforms neglect certain communities—specifically, marginalized communities—while catering to different audiences (Rodriguez & Ofori, 2001). Chinmay, a journalist working for the past twenty-five years for various English newspapers, shares similar sentiments about the focus of journalists on their core audiences. English newspapers and television channels in India cater to the urban population, who are interested mostly in news related to them. So, rape and sexual violence that happens in a city or closer to a city gets a lot of coverage in the English press. There are countless cases like that of Jyoti Singh, which have happened and they are still happening in Tamil Nadu, but no one sheds a tear for them."

There are no candlelight marches or other protest marches for these victims; they are not celebrated, and no one takes up their cause. Chinmay goes on to say: "Sometimes we write about them, but they don't get the same prominence as other cases. No one writes posts on them; neither do they post Facebook messages, nor are hashtags created for them. And often, there are no follow-ups in these cases; eventually, they get lost in the news cycle and from public memory."

It is part of a global issue with news coverage in general that marginalized populations do not get as much coverage as the majority. Anti-rape activists in rural areas work relentlessly without public or political acknowledgment; hence they must work with greater force. Rural feminist activists also face the most resistance and gatekeeping from policy makers, social media platforms like Facebook and Twitter, and renowned activists. One of the rural-based feminist activists said, "We want to apply for funding for our activism, but we have neither the resources nor the help from activist groups for whom we do workshops." Another rural anti-rape activism group, Red Brigade, based in Lucknow, had to hire a digital strategist to help the group manage its online activism. Its Facebook page had previously been deleted for posting photographs of a molestation incident, but it has now hired a professional digital strategist for its digital communication and advocacy.

In this study, I focused on whose stories appear on social media or mass media platforms. In the process, I learned that not everyone's story gets the same kind of attention, whether in mainstream media or social media. Even the international media focuses on the stories that have already been amplified in social media and domestic media, further focusing on the same rapes and sexual assaults and neglecting the others. While I was writing this chapter, there was news of a gang-rape victim from Uttar Pradesh being attacked for the fourth time with acid in July 2017. She had previously been attacked by rapists in March 2017 on a train ("Gang-rape Survivor," 2017). She was gang-raped in 2008 in her village over a property dispute and was physically attacked in 2011 and in 2013 ("Gangrape Survivor

Attacked with Acid," 2017). However, her repeated physical and acid attacks did not merit any social media or hashtag movements. Although they were covered in detail by the English and regional news media across all platforms, they were not addressed by policy makers in the State Assembly or by the minister by asking law enforcement to take swift action against the perpetrators. Nor was there any protest or outrage by the public to influence the political leaders to take action. I can only speculate that since the victim was raped and assaulted over and over again in a smaller city, her ordeal was not "important enough" for a social media campaign and slipped through the gap between news media and social media.

Despite this incident taking place in the interior of the country, it has, surprisingly, received a great deal of attention from the mass media. One of the reasons could be the repeated attacks on the victim and her resilience. Another reason could be political. The state of Uttar Pradesh recently held state-level elections (known as assembly elections in India), and the victim had met the newly elected chief minister in March 2017 after she was attacked the third time (A. Pandey, 2017). From the data gathered in this study, I assume that the mass media treated this as political news. Sanjib, a Mumbai-based multiplatform journalist, said, "Rape incidents are covered by political and crime beat journalists. Then, depending on the nature of the case, it gets assigned to female journalists." Hitendra and Pratap, both Delhi-based journalists with thirty years of experience, agree with Sanjib that rape issues often become political. Political leaders use rape and sexual assault incidents as campaign rhetoric and get involved in blaming the government in power, which is covered by the media. Instead of showing leadership by creating policies or creating mandatory training programs for law enforcement officials, political leaders always take the opportunity to campaign against the opposing parties. They fail to "turn the searchlight inwards," as Mahatma Gandhi said.

Researchers have argued that rape is a part of political narrative in the media, when it is framing rape as a sex crime with a political agenda (Hirschauer, 2014; Coulter & Meyer, 2015). This is also evident from some of the news reports published after Jyoti Singh's rape and subsequent death, which equated rape and violence against women with a political news story: "Law-makers who have been shedding tears over the Delhi gang rape do not match their words with action. While MPs and MLAs of all political hues demanded the death penalty for the accused" (Dhawani, 2012).

5 · MOVING FORWARD
Learning from Anti-rape Feminist Movements

The concluding chapter will focus on the lessons learned from the rural feminist activists in India and the transnational hashtag movements. It will also conclude with the findings and answers to the question of how anti-rape and sexual harassment activism can proceed beyond the watershed activism related to Jyoti Singh in India and Hollywood in the United States. Finally, through this chapter, I engage with Trinh T. Minh-ha's belief, in the context of her documentary *Reassemblage* (1983): "I do not intend to speak about. Just speak nearby." As in my previous work, through this book, I do not intend to speak about the media engagement of anti-rape feminist activists in India; rather, I speak by being near the activists, journalists, culture, and the situation and not imposing my meaning on the participants.

From 2011 to 2013, globally, there was a rise in various social and political movements, such as Occupy Wall Street, the anti-corruption movement, and the anti-street-harassment movement, and scholars, activists, and journalists credited the rise of social and political movements to social media platforms. Whether it was the Arab Spring, Occupy Wall Street, the Ukrainian protest, the Indian anti-corruption protest, or others, the buzzword was social media protests. However, the activists who spearheaded these movements are gradually coming to terms with the challenges of social media activism. Wael Ghonim, the activist who started the Arab Spring, shared his experience in a TED talk in 2016 about the internet, in which he expressed his cynicism: "I once said, 'If you want to liberate a society, all you need is the Internet.' I was wrong. . . . The same tool that united us to topple dictatorship eventually tore us apart."

Similarly, after the #MeToo and #MeTooIndia movements reached their pinnacle in 2017 and 2018, respectively, there was a relative lull in 2019, raising the possibility that the impact of the movement is waning (Khan & Pathak, 2019). On July 21, 2019, the Quint and the Wire reported that the Indian government panel on sexual harassment and abuse that was created nine months after the hashtag movement in October 2018 was dissolved without any announcement. Iyer (2019) writes: "Women we spoke to said the government's prompt response and acknowledgment in October 2018 was greeted with hope, but that their anticipation has turned to anger. It has been nine months since the committee was formed and six months since they had to submit recommendations. At the same time, the number of complaints and frequency at which women call out sexual harassers on social media has reduced. In light of this, *The Quint* filed RTIs to investigate the committee's contribution to the #MeToo movement."

Surprisingly, there has been little to no coverage of this in the leading English newspapers, nor any social media outrage over the decision. Some members of the Twitterati expressed their disappointment with the decision; for example, Nivedith Alva, a television show producer, tweeted "Govt dissolves the #MeToo panel it set up last October. Nothing on what came of it. + Our media has forgotten all the people, especially those in Bollywood, who were named. I'm guessing sometime this year—they will all be back in business like nothing happened" (Alva, 2019).

The disappointment about the movement and its impact is not limited to just social media observers and the public; it is also evident in the survivors. Tanushree Dutta, the Bollywood actress who renewed the #MeTooIndia movement in 2018 by going public with her sexual harassment experience in Bollywood with another actor, Nana Patekar, was disappointed when the charges against Patekar were dropped by the Mumbai police. In response to the acquittal, Dutta shared her statement through WhatsApp, with journalists stating that she was exhausted from fighting the corrupt system, her oppressors, and bullies (Gandhi, 2019).

A standard complaint about any hashtag movement, including #MeToo, is that it is all talk with negligible action (Wilhelm, 2019). Why the sudden cynicism about a tool that until recently was viewed as the savior of marginalized and oppressed communities? Other feminist writers and activists, such as Lindy West, are increasingly identifying the challenges and concerns of social media activism. In an opinion piece for *The New York Times*, published on February 1, 2018, titled "I Quit Twitter and It Feels Great," she writes about her decision to quit Twitter in 2017 due to constant abuse on the microblogging platform and the inability of the platform to reform itself. There is no denying that Twitter provides a space for writers, media professionals and activists to communicate, connect, and advocate. However, online harassment whether on Twitter or other platforms is compounded by the identity politics of race, gender, and sexual orientation. West (2018) clarifies that it's a no-win situation, "I shouldn't have had to walk away from all that because for Twitter to take a firm stance against neo-Nazism might have cost it some incalculable sliver of profit. No one should. Sure, as in everything, global culture change would have been better. But I didn't have global culture change, and I'm better equipped to fight for global culture change now that I'm not locked in eternal whack-a-mole with a sea of angry boy-men, an unknown percentage of which are probably robots" (West, 2018).

Activists and citizens are increasingly discussing the pitfalls of social media activism. In the context of the Standing Rock digital activism, Amanda Jones (2016) wrote for the *Huffington Post* about the superficiality of the exercise: "Sure, it is great for garnering attention about an issue (which is important), but it is ultimately just fads that suddenly boom in popularity but die out as quickly as they appear. People mindlessly join in before swiftly moving on to the next campaign in vogue and abandoning the previous one."

Harry Cheadle, in his article published on January 7, 2017, in VICE, also identified the issues with which both Twitter and Facebook were grappling: "Facebook is filled with fake news stories and hoaxes, and its latest feature, Facebook Live, most recently captured a horrific alleged hate crime. Nearly everything you read on social media—down to even a 'liberal tears' mug that was promoted all over Twitter last month—is somehow a lie."

What we are now experiencing is the dark side of citizen empowerment; tools and platforms that were once perceived as positive now have both positive and negative consequences. This undermines the positive framing of the social media platforms. Wael Ghonim identified the following issues of social media activism in his TED talk in 2016:

- We don't know how to deal with rumors—they spread too fast.
- We tend to only communicate with people with whom we agree.
- Online discussions quickly descend into angry mobs.
- We are forced to jump to conclusions.
- Our digital experiences favor broadcasting over engagement, posts over discussions.
- We talk at, not with.

Ghonim identified multiple issues with social media–based activism, including the tendency to communicate in silos, which Eli Pariser describes as the *filter bubble* problem in his research (2011). Other studies have identified the same thing: that people, not social media platforms, organize people. There is no denying that social media platforms are important tools, but they are supplemental tools in organizing activism, and not the main platform. This needs to be understood by both activists and citizens, along with the gap between awareness and action.

An article in the *Times of India*, written by Pradeep Thakuri on June 24, 2017, concentrated on the plight of rape victims in India. Headlined "5 Years on, It's the Same Ordeal for Nirbhayas," the news article described the challenges faced by rape survivors and victims in the capital city of Delhi. What is fascinating in this article is the consistent focus on the status quo of the system of the victims of sexual violence and survivors, the absence of rape crisis centers, resistance in filing FIRs, and the persistence of other legal and medical issues. Although Thakuri did not venture into the watershed moments of the protests and policy changes that happened after Nirbhaya's rape and murder, or the fact that even after five years the harassment continues, the author does accept that the 2012 Delhi gang-rape case was a milestone. Scholars and journalists (Danish, 2013; Dey, 2014; Jolly, 2016) also agree that the 2012 Delhi gang-rape case is a watershed moment because of the policy changes in rape and sexual harassment laws achieved through the implementation of the Justice Verma Commission recommendations.

In 1996, a 16-year-old girl was kidnapped and gang-raped by 42 men over 45 days in Suryanelli, Kerala. This heinous incident is known as the Suryanelli rape case. It was not until 2014 that some of the perpetrators were punished by the Supreme Court of India. The Suryanelli victim has repeatedly pointed to indifference from the state and the media. "The survivor of the Suryanelli rape case lamented that 'no one ever gave me a name like Nirbhaya or Amanat. . . . I will never be the nation's pride or the face of women wronged'" (Losh, 2014). This clearly indicates that there is selective outrage by the media, in which "victims" are carefully selected to lead the coverage and the agenda (Arora, 2014). Much of the outrage also depends on the Indian media system.

Six years after Jyoti Singh's heinous rape and murder, Sanjali, a sixteen-year-old girl, was raped and burned alive on a wintry afternoon in Agra, a small town in Uttar Pradesh, the largest state in India. Sanjali's rape and murder received only limited newspaper coverage in the two highest-circulation newspapers in India over two weeks. There were no candlelight marches and no celebrities tweeting #JusticeForSanjali on Facebook or Twitter.

Since September 2018, #MeTooIndia has been a constant topic of conversation on online platforms and newspapers, but these conversations have not been inclusive.

I included the functionality and scope of online activism in chapters 2 and 3 while discussing the successes and failures of online hashtag feminist activism, the algorithmic focus of social media platforms, and the impact of misinformation on anti-rape and sexual harassment activism. Algorithms tend to focus on urban-based rapes, sexual harassment, and sexual assaults. Social media platforms have often been accused of creating silos and causing people to live in bubbles, but they do give space to marginalized communities and others to create and have conversations about taboo topics. However, they are still restrictive, and algorithmic power also influences social media activism (Treré, 2018). Harlow and Guo (2014) note, "It is important to explore the usefulness and potential of Information Communication Technologies (ICTs) for activism (Cleaver, 1998; Diani, 1999). Employing this paradigm, journalists focus on numbers,

Moving Forward   101

spectacles, or dramatic actions, rather than the message underlying the action (Watkins, 2001). To counter mainstream media's misinformation, activists often turn to alternative media (Downing, 2001)" (p. 465).

The relationship between social media networks and mainstream mass media has the potential to create an interdependent agenda.

INTERDEPENDENT AGENDA BUILDING IN ANTI-RAPE AND SEXUAL HARASSMENT ACTIVISM

Many incidences of sexual assault and harassment from 2017 until 2019 demonstrate how interdependent agenda building can work in the context of feminist digital activism in a digitally emerging country like India. Analyzing these cases provides insights into how information about sexual assault and harassment incidents is disseminated to the public, law enforcement, and policy makers, as well as how it feeds into citizen engagement on such incidents. Right now there is a gap in the exchange of information among journalists, activists, policy makers, and the public on issues of rape and sexual assault. Similar examples of rape and sexual assault do not result in similar levels of public outrage and political action: convictions do not take place in all rape, molestation, or sexual assault allegations; justice is not delivered in all rape, molestation, and sexual assault allegations; and the conviction rate for rape and sexual assault is low relative to the number of reports filed in India, as demonstrated in figure 5.1. This provides a visualization of the existing gap between filing a report and convicting the offender in sexual harassment, identifying the gap between social activism and policy making.

Mainstream media coverage of rape and sexual assault and the use of social media platforms for anti-rape activism operate in silos. Other than the protests in response to Jyoti Singh's rape and murder, the public outrage, discussion, and impact on mainstream media and social media have been muted. After Jisha's

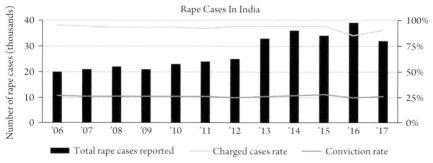

FIGURE 5.1. Comparative data of rape reporting, charging, and conviction from 2006 to 2017 based on the National Crime Records Bureau report

rape and murder, no official action was taken against the law enforcement officials who failed to take her complaint the first time around. There was an increase in the number of complaints of sexual assault and rape filed with the police in 2013; many attributed this phenomenon to Jyoti Singh's rape and murder and the Criminal Act Amendment of 2013. However, it is not surprising to note that, from 2015 onward, the annual NCRB reports have shown a decline in the number of cases of rape, sexual assault, and molestation registered. The number of rape and sexual assault convictions continued to be low in 2013, 2016, and 2018. Journalists and activists have pointed out that law enforcement officials are quick to register and conclude the case without following protocol, resulting in a loss of evidence and information. The gap between policies, implementing the policies, understanding the policies, and making the public aware can be reduced if the mainstream news media and the social media groups work together.

In August 2015, an American tourist was sexually harassed in Mumbai. The survivor took to Twitter and tagged the chief minister of the state to narrate her experience. The news media immediately picked up on the news and provided consistent coverage. There were swift actions against the perpetrators. Since an American tourist was sexually harassed, there was comparatively more focus in the news. There was a combined effort between social media platforms and mainstream news media, which created both a public and a political agenda and resulted in tangible actions.

The lack of concerted effort between social media and news media in sexual harassment and sexual abuse creates a gap in public and political agenda building.

On New Year's Eve in 2016, more than fifteen women were sexually harassed during a celebration on the streets of Bangalore. The number of women harassed was not officially confirmed; the unofficial number came from some of the harassed women and their friends, who decided to write about their ordeal on their personal Facebook pages. These were shared by feminist groups on their pages, and in a few days, they went viral. Chaitali Wasnik, a wedding photographer, who was groped and molested, wrote on her Facebook page that the police did nothing to help her, but that she kicked and punched the perpetrator. She did not mention whether she later filed a formal police complaint. The police reported to the media that no complaints were filed against any perpetrators. However, after the initial reports became public, the police and some of the elected ministers of the city rejected the claims of the women who had been molested. The mainstream news media reported on the molestations only on January 4, 2017, four days after the incident.

What is important here is that the police and political leadership did not acknowledge the harassment, let alone act on the allegations. The police did not open a case, file any FIRs, or even check the closed-circuit television (CCTV) footage to verify the claims of the women immediately after the incident. The first complaint was filed after four days, with the publication of the news in the media. In fact, instead of asking the police to investigate the matter, one political leader of the ruling party of Karnataka, a southern state, indulged in a blame game by accusing the women of having loose morals and following a Western lifestyle of going to clubs and pubs late at night ("Women Molested," 2017). The political leaders from the government and the opposition dismissed the social media allegations and the subsequent outrage in the social media platforms. Demanding a full-blown investigation on the basis of social media allegations may have been a stretch, but at the same time, the claims of sexual harassment should not have been dismissed outright. There are other ways of verifying claims, such as checking CCTV footage in the public places where the molestations happened, which is what the police eventually did.

Finally, after a week, when mainstream television and newspapers started reporting the incident by publishing photographs of the molestations, the perpetrators, and partial photographs of the victims with the police, along with eyewitness accounts from Facebook posts and editorial columns by activists, the police responded to the allegations of molestation made by the women. The mainstream news media covered the mass molestation in detail and even interviewed some of the survivors. This consistent reporting by the mainstream media on the incident forced the police to act and identify the perpetrators via CCTV television footage. The interdependent connection between social and mainstream media helped the activists and victims to make a case against the perpetrators.

A second incident shows the failure to act when there is a lack of concerted effort between social media and the news media. After the #MeTooIndia movement was revived in 2018, many women working in news and entertainment media in India started sharing their accounts of sexual harassment and sexual abuse on social media platforms, including Facebook and Twitter. While most women were sharing their ordeals on social media platforms, a couple of women journalists shared their experiences of being sexually harassed in a leading Bengali newsroom through an independent digital news portal, *The Bengal Story*. Two journalists at the newspaper *Ananda Bazar Patrika* shared how they were repeatedly sexually harassed in the paper's newsroom in Kolkata (Pallavi Majumdar by Sanjay Sikdar in 2008, and Saberee Gupta by Debdut Ghoshthakur in 2015). Both women complained to Shiuli Biswas in the human resources department, but received an unsympathetic reception: Pallavi was forced to resign and was escorted out of the office forty minutes after filing her complaint, and Saberee was transferred to another department (Gupta, 2018; Majumdar, 2018).

When Majumdar was sexually harassed, there were no social media platforms or blogging sites where she could express her thoughts about her ordeal or become part of a hashtag movement. Majumdar was forced out of the newsroom because she complained of the harassment and there was no redressal. The following is an excerpt from her conversation with the publisher and the news editor after she filed the complaint (Majumdar, 2018):

His first question was, why did you lodge a complaint?

JOURNALIST: Mr. Bandopadhyay advised me to.
BABU: Who is he to advise? He is no one. Who cares what he said?
JOURNALIST: Sir, he is our News Editor. I confided in him first, and he suggested that I lodge an official complaint.
BABU: So? Don't you have a judgment of your own? Why are you following his?
JOURNALIST: Sir, I felt his advice was justified as the harassment was getting intolerable for me.
BABU: Really?
JOURNALIST: Yes, Sir.
BABU: But I heard you do not have any proof.
JOURNALIST: How can one have proof of sexual harassment?
BABU (WITH A SMILE): Then how can one think that there can be a redressal?
JOURNALIST (TRYING TO SWALLOW HER TEARS): Then why have you created the harassment cell, Sir?
BABU: Because it is a corporate need of the time, lady. Just like the useless judicial system we have in our country! We have courts, lawyers, judges . . . But how many people get justice? Almost none. A sexual harassment cell is like that. It is created because today's corporate structure demands it. That's all, my dear.

All this while Bandopadhyay sat there looking intently at his mobile phone. He spoke no word, nor did he look at the woman once. She was feeling miserable by now; the impact of Babu's words had crushed her confidence.

Babu went on saying: If you have a fight with your brother, if your dad slaps you once, do you go to the police station? No, you settle it among yourselves instead. Then why did you go for a complaint here? Isn't this your family? Withdraw the complaint. And do it fast. Just mention that it was a misunderstanding, and you do not wish to continue with this trouble. I can get you transferred to another department if you like.

JOURNALIST: What if I do not withdraw the complaint? And I do not want a transfer either, Sir, because I love my job and I get along well with my other colleagues in the department.
BABU: Then the inquiry will continue, and it will ultimately prove you a liar and you shall be forced to write an apology. Would that be a more respectable solution for you?

Majumdar resigned immediately after this conversation, but there was no discussion within the media community in the city. There was active gatekeeping by the news media, which buried this particular sexual harassment incident. As mentioned above, Majumdar's harassment was not the only incident of sexual harassment within a newsroom that was suppressed: in the same newsroom, in 2015, Gupta filed a complaint against the chief reporter after repeated sexual harassment. She was immediately transferred to a tabloid newsmagazine and, as a result, left her job after a month and a half (Gupta, 2018). She gave the following account of her experience:

> He would also enjoy cracking bawdy jokes, using filthy language all the time. He would say women were not good as employees because they would soon get married and then get pregnant. When a horrific incident took place in Barasat, in the northern fringes of Kolkata, in which a young man was killed trying to protect his elder sister from molesters, the ABP's male reporters in their evening meeting discussed that it was "normal" for men to feel the urge to touch women. One evening, Ghoshthakur and I were taking the same office pool car home because we both lived in south Kolkata and office cars were allotted accordingly. Ghoshthakur pinched my buttocks the moment I got into the car after him. I was numb with shock and jumped out immediately. I decided to sit by the side of the driver on the way home. Next morning, I reported the matter to our News Editor, who was Debdut Ghoshthakur's boss. He laughed. That was his first reaction. When I asked him why he was laughing, he stopped and said he would look into the matter. But he did nothing. (Gupta, 2018)

Again, there was no social media outrage or news media coverage of the incident. Without the intervention of social media platforms, the news media was successful in controlling coverage of such incidents of sexual assault and harassment.

For the past five years, a former colleague of mine has been fighting against sexual harassment at the newsroom where we worked together. In 2015, Nasreen Khan (2018) filed a complaint of sexual harassment against her editor, which resulted in her dismissal from the newsroom. It was not until the #MeTooIndia movement in 2018 that Khan wrote openly about her harassment and eventual dismissal on the news portal she founded. After sharing her post on Facebook, at least two more women employees who worked with the same editor publicly shared on Facebook their experiences of sexual harassment and eventual resignation from the newsroom. Khan was interviewed by other news media organizations, and these interviews, together with the Facebook posts by the other women, were vital information for the executive management observers at the organization, ultimately leading to the editor's transfer from his position. But, as has been the case for other survivors, it has been a lonely battle for Khan (2018), who recalled: "Much to my embarrassment, I broke down before her and decided to stop my efforts there. I did all I could to protect my self-respect and dignity. Now it was taking a toll on me. I could not afford my aged parents or my young child to see me like this. I had to move on. I did and switched careers. . . . His last victim had got in touch with me seeking guidance. Speaking from my experience, I told her to move on and focus on her career."

Khan was able to share her ordeal, which resulted in some action due to the concerted effort of both social media sites and mainstream news media outlets. After years of fighting for justice, she succeeded in bringing to light the continued sexual harassment.

There are many other sexual harassment and abuse survivors who have anonymously shared their ordeals in blogs. In 2017, a twenty-four-year-old woman wrote a blog under the pseudonym "India's Fowler" accusing Arunabh Kumar, the CEO of the production company TVF (The Viral Fever) in India, of sexual harassment and intimidation. It was published on March 12, 2017, by Medium, a blog site that publishes original content. On March 14, 2017, most leading newspapers started reporting on the matter. The publication of the blog in the newspapers encouraged other women employees of TVF who had also been harassed by Kumar to come forward. Some posted their experiences on their Facebook pages, and others commented anonymously on the original blog post.

A leading English news channel in India, New Delhi Television Limited (popularly known as NDTV), reported that fifty women sent direct messages to a particular Twitter handle sharing their experiences of harassment by Kumar. This Twitter handle, which has been locked since April 2017, had shared the first blog post by "India's Fowler." Meanwhile, the accused CEO and the production company denounced the claims made by the woman ("India's Fowler") on their Twitter feeds and Facebook pages. TVF released a statement defending the CEO as a member of its team, claiming: "The article is completely ludicrous and defamatory against TVF (The Viral Fever) and its team. All the allegations made against TVF and its team in the article are categorically false, baseless, and unverified. . . . We will leave no stone unturned to find the author of the article and bring them to severe justice for making such false allegations" (The Viral Fever, 2017).

The blog published on Medium by "India's Fowler" was shared by other online news websites such as Quartz, Mashable, Newsminute, and others. In addition to the fifty women who shared their experiences of their ordeals through a direct message to the Twitter handle, two other women, Reema Sengupta and Reshma Patra, wrote Facebook posts supporting the allegations of "India's Fowler" and alleging similar harassment by Kumar (Bhattacharya, 2017). Their Facebook posts were widely shared, and within two days, the mainstream media started reporting on the case; momentum to demand action began building through editorials, reports, and parallel social media outrage. Of course, the

Moving Forward   107

fact that the blog was written anonymously gave many the ammunition to doubt its authenticity. The mainstream media specifically mentioned in the coverage that it was not possible to verify the accuracy of the original post by "India's Fowler," and the news media did not interview any of the fifty women who alleged harassment by Kumar. Some of the women identified themselves publicly by posting personal details such as their first and last names, photographs, and professions on their Facebook pages. However, while all the news articles I read on the accusations against Kumar had screengrabs of these women, none of them had interviewed the identified women, despite the ease of contacting them via Facebook.

Within a week, the mainstream news media covered the case prominently and consistently, as most leading English newspapers covered the allegations of sexual harassment. The general trends initially focused on the allegations made by "India's Fowler" and the existence of workplace harassment in organizations, including start-ups. Besides the news media coverage, there was also social media outrage, including outrage from feminists and feminist activists, which forced the production company to tone down its initial response and issue a second statement to a leading newspaper in India, *Daily News Analysis*, on March 17, 2017. The following is an excerpt from this press statement, demonstrating the shift in tone from dismissing the molestation accusation to agreeing to set up a committee:

> We did send out an instant response, which may have been a bit too quick and emotional (*sic*). We recognize that we should have handled that response better. However, it is a fact that we have found no records of any such person on our payroll in that given time period, as described in the blog. Even as we were dealing with the first episode, several other allegations surfaced soon thereafter. Please know that we are sincerely looking into each one of them. We are committed to getting to the bottom of these allegations. Many of you have asked, so we would like to confirm that yes, we have an ICC Committee set up in each location. (Corporate Communication Team, The Viral Fever, March 2017)

After the sexual harassment cases became public, a lawyer filed a third-party police complaint against Kumar. Third-party police complaints can be filed by any individual or organization other than the victim/complainant (Kalkod, 2010).

In a more recent incident, in June 2019, Ushoshi Sengupta, a former beauty pageant winner, was molested by a group of seven perpetrators while she was a passenger in an Uber vehicle (IANS, 2019). Ushoshi had a hard time lodging a police complaint and took to Facebook to narrate her ordeal ("Kolkata: Former Miss India," 2019). What followed was consistent, in-depth coverage of the incident in the news media, including interviews with her. The social media post, along with the news media coverage, prompted legal and police action, including arresting the perpetrators and suspension of the officer who refused to file Ushoshi's complaint ("Had to Stand Up," 2019).

In all the incidents—the mass molestation on New Year's Eve and the TVF sexual harassment and intimidation case—the police acted only after the incidents received mainstream media coverage. Of course, social media platforms created space for the women to write about their harassment, but the information about the harassment did not make its way to the public until the mainstream media covered the issues. Neither law enforcement nor the police publicly appealed through the media to the victims to register a complaint against the perpetrators. This step could have encouraged more women to file complaints of molestation and sexual assault, but it happened when some women came forward. An appeal from law enforcement would have encouraged more women to come forward and register their complaints.

In the past few years, journalists have been making a concerted effort to locate stories on social media sites; however, verifying the stories on these sites remains a challenge because of the many pseudonymous accounts on social media, which makes tracing a post back to the original source of information difficult. In my interviews, veteran journalists suggested that sources from social media sites should be in addition to the groundwork that journalists do on stories. Younger journalists tend to get information from social media sites such as Twitter and Facebook but do not always verify the claims or information shared on these platforms. Shared content, including videos, memes, and images, on these social media platforms is sometimes created by the users, and it becomes difficult to distinguish between real and contrived posts. During the interviews I conducted, journalists also agreed that it is difficult and time-consuming to verify information from social media sites.

Activists, especially individuals who have no or limited access to the internet, need to depend on the mainstream media to reach the public. This interdependence between social media and the news media may act in combination to reach the audience and policy makers. The audience is known to seek out agendas from various forms of media depending on their cognition; this concept is defined as agendamelding (McCombs, 2014). McCombs (2014) developed the concept of agendamelding based on the development of an agenda formed unconsciously, where individuals borrow from a variety of agendas to create and enforce a public agenda, albeit unconsciously. Agendamelding also implies that one specific media platform is no longer able to set the agenda. On a similar note, Bekkers et al. (2011) propose that the internet facilitated a paradigm shift in the macro- and meso-mobilization processes of media agenda setting by focusing on micro-mobilization by small groups and individuals. The argument of this study is based on the meso- and micro-mobilization of civic and political movements developing through the internet, where information flows from the micro media to the mass media. Bekkers et al.'s proposition was developed when social media networks began to make inroads into mainstream activism and journalism. The thesis was that the new web technologies would influence and mediate the course of political agenda setting, and that the crossover effects from the micro media to the mass media would eventually become possible through social and political movements. Similarly, Meraz (2009) focuses her study on the diminishing agenda-setting power of the traditional media. The mainstream mass media is no longer the primary or only source of information for the public to influence its agenda. This challenges the gatekeeping function of the mainstream mass media and distributes the power to set the public agenda to political bloggers, activists, and community advocates. Meraz (2009, 2011) and J. Lee (2007) found that political bloggers are becoming a decisive force in directing the media agenda.

J. Lee (2007) connects both blogging and mainstream news in setting the agenda. The study investigates the relationship between the blog agenda and the mainstream media agenda in the coverage of the 2004 U.S. presidential election. J. Lee posits that, instead of fragmentation of public opinion due to the distinct agendas of bloggers and mainstream news, there can be a collaboration between the two. Optimists predict that interactive or two-way communication empowers people to select their own agenda, whereas pessimists argue that a fragmented audience will no longer be able to converse on the same social issues and reach consensus on them. These apparently contradictory arguments are based on the assumption of a heterogeneous media agenda to which most people are exposed.

As discussed previously, McCombs's (2014) concept of agendamelding is based on the unconscious borrowing of agendas from different sources. However, it is manifest that this borrowing not always be unconscious, particularly in the presence of social media networks. In most cases, the citizenry consciously identifies their individual opinion with the public agenda and media agenda setting.

The concept of gatekeeping is described as the flow of news from one media organization to another through a series of gatekeepers before it reaches the public (McCombs, 2014, p. 57). Gatekeeping is a "regime of control" over what content is allowed to emerge from the newsroom and enter public circulation (Bruns, 2005, p. 11). "A journalistic gatekeeper determines not just the quantity of information that reaches the public but also its quality according to particular definitions, shared among members of an interpretive community, of what news is or should be" (Singer, 2014, p. 60). The cascading model of top-down information flow from the media to the public is diminishing, much like the gatekeeping function of the elite group of journalists and political leaders, who "framed and transferred" the agenda to the public. Singer (2014) argues that journalists have repositioned the gatekeeping role; they are passing off to online users a growing range of related tasks. The users, as mentioned by Singer, become the "secondary" gatekeepers by participating in social media networks. However, Singer does not attribute to the public the agency to become the "primary gatekeepers." I speculate that in the present context—in cases of activism—the public has somewhat assumed the role of self-gatekeeping, which emboldens the bottom-up approach. Although the concept of gatekeeping is historically connected to the effects of mass communication, digital media is reshaping the concept by transforming a mass audience into smaller and atomized audiences. The research of Wu, Hoffman, Winter, and Watts (2011) pointed to this change, showing that the top ten most-followed users on Twitter were not corporations or media organizations but individuals who communicate directly with their followers via messages, which were usually written by them or their publicists. They thus bypass the intermediation of what are usually understood as gatekeepers (Bastos, Raimundo, and Travitzki, 2013).

During the interviews for this book, both journalists and activists agreed that citizens were aware of what was happening and even participating by sharing news links, memes, hashtags, and other media; but at the same time, they wondered if the citizens were able to send a strong message of activism through their participation in social media platforms. They questioned how many took concrete action to influence the mass media and other stakeholders to bring about a change.

Scholars and activists are increasingly starting to recognize the issues of dependence on social media platforms for activism. Some of these issues helped me to structure the recommendations of this study and, as an outcome, to create an app that could be used by both feminist activists and journalists to bridge the existing gap between rape incidents and reporting.

Activists have identified trolling and silos as some of the issues with social media activism, but how do academics define the issues? Mihailidis (2017) identified the following issues of social media activism:

- Commodification and spectacle: It is a myth that social media platforms such as Facebook, Twitter, Snapchat, and others are not commodified. YouTube channels, Facebook pages, and Instagram influencers are all examples of commercialization. The added pressure of spectacle on social media and focus on the number of likes, followers, and subscribers leads to further commercialization through monetization of posts. The platforms also promote the use of filters and other enhancements, which require internet band-width and skills to use them. In the context of this book, many subaltern feminist activists in India do not have such skills, thus failing to create a spectacle and capture the attention of the mass media. The dependence of mass media on spectacle tends to take attention away from the main issue. Social media platforms only work when spectacle is included.

- Agency gap: The lack of spectacle and commodification leads to the gap in agency and influencing citizens. The increasing gap between awareness, participation, and taking action impacts meaningful engagement and agenda-building. (Mihailidis, 2017).

In a digitally emerging country like India, subaltern feminist activists may own smartphones and have access to digital media, but digital literacy is low. Consequently, creating mostly text content is a challenge for these activists. If they network with journalists, they can get their stories out. But as much as journalists want to tell the activists' stories, other factors interfere, such as limited space for publication or breaking news. Here, social media platforms can be helpful in amplifying the stories and forcing the mainstream media to take note. This is where the interdependence of agenda building becomes important and necessary.

CONCLUSION

Social media platforms have influenced the way citizens participate in social movements and engage with news and issues. In the recent past, survivors and victims of sexual harassment and assault have used social media platforms globally to amplify their abuse and structural problems related to sexual violence. However, recent news reports have identified that anti-sexual-assault movements grapple with the issue of consistency (Casselman, Tankersley, & Smialek, 2020). For instance, the women's march, which started in January 2017, is struggling to survive three years later in the United States. It is not much different in other countries. #MeTooIndia re-emerged with force in 2018, which led to the establishment of a government working group; however, the working group was later dismantled, and #MeTooIndia did not find a space during the 2019 election campaign.

In February 2020, Harvey Weinstein was sentenced to prison for repeated sexual abuse of women who have worked with him. There is no doubt that #MeToo had an impact on both the charges against Weinstein and the sentence he received. Finally, a long-kept secret had emerged in the public sphere. However, we cannot ignore the results of the journalistic investigations by Kantor and Twohey (2019) to bring to light several other victims and survivors who have stayed away from sharing their plight on social media platforms.

On the other hand, a year after the #MeToo movement, most of the perpetrators at news organizations or in the movie industry have "resumed" working. Bhattacharya (2019) lists the number of accused Bollywood producers, actors, and directors who have resumed working since accusations of sexual abuse surfaced, but the women are still bearing the brunt. Bhattacharya outlines how one journalist, Priya Ramani, is fighting a lone battle in the courtroom of defamation with M. J. Akbar, a former editor, journalist, and central minister accused of sexual abuse in a newsroom.

There is no denying that the hashtag made sexual abuse and harassment in the media a public conversation in India, but there was limited involvement by the mainstream media on investigating and reporting on the issue. This attitude limited to an extent the reach and engagement of the #MeTooIndia movement. There were multiple follow-up news stories assessing the limited scope of the movement. Meenakshi Menon wrote one such piece in *Business Today* on the little action taken against the perpetrators. "The #Metoo movement has also raised more questions and concerns than the solutions it has offered" (M. Menon, 2019). The news coverage has focused on the misuse of the movement. The coverage has overlooked the harassment of the victims and survivors in precarious newsrooms, whose stories were never heard. Perhaps following Gandhi's advice of turning the searchlight inward, focusing on the investigative pieces, and introspecting the harassment would help the movement.

Social media sites have created their own spaces to build an agenda on important issues with the participation of citizens and activists, but the mainstream media is needed to bridge this gap between online and offline engagement. A news article published by Reuters in December 2018 asked about the involvement and the possibility of a #MeToo movement in Indian politics (Banerji, 2018). Indian politicians have been restrained on #MeTooIndia, unlike with Nirbhaya or Asifa or many other such unfortunate incidents. One of the reasons behind this is the accusations of sexual harassment against their colleagues.

There is no doubt that there was restrained coverage, qualitatively and quantitatively, particularly as far as Indian-language newspapers are concerned. It was not surprising that the discussion on sexual harassment moved from safe workplace conditions to a backlash against women and male supervisors avoiding mentoring female team members. The focus of the discussion changed from a structural issue to an individual responsibility and concern. Sexual harassment and abuse became specific to the incident and not structural. It reminds me of a conversation I had with an anti-rape feminist activist, that the public knows only the tip of the iceberg; it is a much bigger issue that has penetrated neither the news media nor the social media platforms. If the citizens were aware of the importance of the issue, we would have seen increased engagement, and public policies to curb sexual abuse.

As academics, we cannot neglect the fact that victims and survivors of sexual abuse are hesitant to come forward because of the social, legal, and political support system. There is no doubt that social media empowers the victims and survivors to know about the others and share their predicaments, but it also puts some victims and survivors in a precarious position. Not everyone is able to share their abuse on social media platforms, owing to issues of access, living in proximity to their abusers, and other societal pressure. This is where the role of

Moving Forward 113

journalists and newsrooms becomes paramount; investigating and publishing allegations of rape and sexual harassment is vital to building the public agenda. A quick search on Lexis Nexis for the *Times of India* in the calendar year generated 233 news articles on sexual harassment and 55 on rape. That's a total of 288 news articles in one calendar year, which roughly translates to less than one story a day. However, according to the statistics, about 89 rapes happen every day in India (NCRB, 2019).[1] This gap between the actual incidence and news reporting needs to be closed, which is possible by interdependent agenda building.

There are still so many survivors and victims who have not been heard in the news media or on social media. Their experiences and quest for justice and the public agenda have slipped into the gap of underreporting and no access to social media platforms. So how do we ensure that, as an organic movement, the public agenda is inclusive of these experiences in public conversation? Public and political policy creation is possible when both the news media and social media are inclusive in hearing the victims and survivors. As users, audiences, and scholars, we cannot deny that both platforms have pitfalls. It is no less than a herculean task to make sure that the anti-rape and sexual assault movement stays afloat and does not fall into the gap between the news media and social media. Bearing in mind the interdependent relationship between the transnational anti-rape feminist movements and the rural feminist movement in India, and the ways they can turn selective media, public, and political outrage of rape and sexual harassment into a consistent approach, I suggest that feminist activists use the multiple platforms of the news media and social media to build a sustained campaign against rape and sexual assault. This will support the building of a public and policy agenda against rape and sexual assault. Social media has fostered a sense of hybrid protest (where social media pressure fosters more traditional media attention), and interdependence of both could build social capital to tackle the issue of violence against women with impunity more broadly.

Engaging in research and writing has been an extension of the catharsis that began in 2015 and continued until 2019, while writing this book. Over the past year, I spoke with several activists and journalists working on issues of rape and sexual harassment and was reminded of Oprah Winfrey's famous quote: "Turn your wounds into wisdom." The anti-rape and sexual harassment feminist activists have indeed turned their wounds into wisdom and applied it to their activism. The journalists and activists have shared their knowledge in this book in order to reach a wider audience. However, I must acknowledge and conclude that these experiences and stories are from a select few; there are many whose stories are not represented. It is only appropriate to conclude with an excerpt from the celebrated feminist writer Amrita Pritam's autobiography, *The Revenue Stamp* (1977): "My story is the story of women in every country. And many more in number are those stories which are not written on paper but are written on the bodies and minds of women."

ACKNOWLEDGMENTS

> We often take for granted the very things that most deserve our gratitude.
> —Cynthia Ozick

I am grateful to the many people in my life who have supported me in writing this book, a labor of love that started as my doctoral research. I want to thank my gods and goddess for keeping me focused and showing me the path to embark on to successfully complete the book.

My family has steadfastly supported me in many ways during this project. I thank my daughter Anahita Guha Choudhury for unconditionally loving me, accommodating my erratic interviewing and writing schedule, and sharing her stickers with me; my parents, Baishakhi Guha and Samir Guha, for encouraging me to keep working by providing logistical and emotional support; and last but not least, my husband, Arya Choudhury, for sharing the family load in every possible way and encouraging me to complete the book.

I am also thankful to those in my life who have supported me in this project and beyond: Supriya Maulick, my best friend, for checking on me frequently from 7,000 miles away; Dr. Linda Steiner, who often asked me about the project and motivated me to keep writing; Dr. Kalyani Chadha, who encouraged me; Dr. Rob Wells, who became my best friend and academic soundboard, for inspiring me to take on this project and periodically asking me about the status of the book; Dr. Radhika Gajjala, my mentor and research collaborator, for always listening to me, encouraging me, and shaping my scholarship; Dr. Paro Pain for her encouragement; my friend Amy Wu for her inspiration; Philip Merrill College of Journalism, University of Maryland, and the Department of Mass Communication, Towson University, for supporting my research; Nicole Solano, my editor, for selecting my project for publication; the anonymous reviewers for their time and feedback, and the editorial and publishing team.

Finally, this project would not have been possible without the labor, knowledge, and passion of my interviewees. We spent hours discussing the role of the media, social media, anti-rape and anti-sexual-harassment activism, feminism, and much more. These candid conversations enlightened me about their struggles, my privileges and struggles, and the public agenda-building efforts on anti-rape activism.

NOTES

1 INTRODUCTION AND HISTORICAL BACKGROUND

1. I discuss four victims in this book. Two of the victims, Jyoti Singh and Pratibha Murthy, are known publicly by their full names, but the other victims are not. To maintain privacy, I use first names only when referring to these other victims.
2. *Nirbhaya* means "fearless" in Hindi. The name Nirbhaya was given by the media to Jyoti Singh, the victim of the infamous Delhi Gang Rape in 2012.

2 FRAMING OF RAPE IN THE NEWS MEDIA AND ITS IMPACT ON FEMINIST ACTIVISM AND JOURNALISTS

1. According to a survey conducted by Pew Research, the hourly wage of female journalists in U.S. newsrooms is 17 percent less than the wage of male journalists. This statistic is based on a survey conducted in 2012. See Willnat, Weaver, & Wilhoit 2017.
2. On December 16, 2012, a paramedical student in Delhi was brutally gang-raped while riding a bus. She died a few days later after succumbing to her injuries. There was a massive protest in response to the rape and assault, and the Indian government set up a judicial committee to look into the incident.

3 THE HEART DOES NOT BLEED FOR EVERYONE

1. Some activists and journalists that I interviewed did not want to be identified. I have used a pseudonym (noted by an asterisk) for these individuals.
2. The Sexual Harassment of Women at Workplace (Prevention, Prohibition and Redressal) Act, 2013 in India was enacted to prevent sexual harassment in the workplace.
3. I choose to use only the first names of the victims and of my interviewees unless their full names are already known publicly.
4. Smaller cities in India are known as tier II cities. The classification is based on the Compensatory City Allowance House Rent Allowance.

4 THE SUCCESSES AND FAILURES OF TRANSNATIONAL HASHTAG MOVEMENTS

1. Bangalore is the hub for IT companies in India. Men and women were equally employed in professional positions; the culture was changing gradually because of the night shifts that IT professionals were required to work.
2. In 2016, the government allocated 200 crore rupees (equivalent to US$310,000) to a fund that was set up in memory of Jyoti Singh Pandey. The Nirbhaya fund, as it is known, supports government initiatives to protect women and children from sexual crimes and provides compensation for survivors.
3. Jisha has been referred to by her first name in the media coverage. There is no reference to her last name.

118   Notes

4. Mathura, a young tribal girl, was raped in 1970 by two police officers in the state of Maharashtra, in western India. The perpetrators were acquitted by the Supreme Court, the highest court in India. However, this judgment led to a huge protest that forced the government to bring about sweeping changes in the existing rape laws, which shifted the burden of proof from the victim to the perpetrator. For more details, see chapter 1.

5 MOVING FORWARD

1. In 2017, 32,559 rapes were reported in India (NCRB, 2019), which results in 89.2 rapes a day.

REFERENCES

After what has happened with Karan Oberoi, it is now time to initiate "MenToo" movement, says Pooja Bedi. (2019, May 8). Retrieved from https://www.outlookindia.com/website/story/society-news-mento-movement-time-for-men-to-step-up/330065

Ahmed, S., Jaidka, K., & Cho, J. (2017). Tweeting India's nirbhaya protest: A study of emotional dynamics in an online social movement. *Social Movement Studies, 16*(4), 447–465

Alat, Z. (2006). News coverage of violence against women. *Feminist Media Studies, 6*(3), 295–314.

Alcoff, L. M. (2012). Feminism: Then and now. *The Journal of Speculative Philosophy, 26*(2), 268–290. Retrieved from https://doi.org/10.5325/jspecphil.26.2.0268

Althaus, S. L., & Tewksbury, D. (2002). Agenda setting and the "new" news: Patterns of issue importance among readers of the paper and online versions of the New York Times. *Communication Research, 29*(2), 180–207. https://doi.org/10.1177/009365020202029002004

Alva, N. (Jul 22, 2019). Govt. dissolves the #metoo panel it set up last October. Retrieved from: https://twitter.com/nivedithalva/status/1153490579621175297

Anasuya, S. I. (2017, October 29). Why the response to a list of sexual harassers has splintered India's feminist movement. Retrieved from https://www.dailyo.in/politics/sexual-harassment-raya-sarkar-kafila-indian-feminism/story/1/20291.html

Andelsman, V. & Mitchelstein, E. (2019) If it bleeds it leads: Coverage of violence against women and sexual and reproductive health in Argentina from 1995 to 2015. *Journalism Practice, 13*(4), 458–475.

Anderson, M. & Toor, S (2018). How social media users have discussed sexual harassment since #MeToo went viral. (2018). Retrieved from https://www.pewresearch.org/fact-tank/2018/10/11/how-social-media-users-have-discussed-sexual-harassment-since-metoo-went-viral/

Andrews, K., & Caren, N. (January 01, 2010). Making the News: Movement Organizations, Media Attention, and the Public Agenda. American Sociological Review, 75, 6, 841–866.

Aneja, K. (2016, May 7). Stop selective outrage over rape. *The Times of India.* Retrieved from http://timesofindia.indiatimes.com/city/bengaluru/Stop-selective-outrage-over-rape/articleshow/52159325.cms

AoIR. (2016). [Ethics graphic]. *AOIR guidelines: Ethical decision making and internet research ethics: 2012.* Retrieved from http://aoir.org/wp-content/uploads/2017/01/aoir_ethics_graphic_2016.pdf

Ardovini-Brooker, J., & Caringella-Macdonald, S. (2002). Media attributions of blame and sympathy in ten rape cases. *The Justice Professional, 15*(1), 3–18.

Arora, N. (2014, December). Delhi: The city of rape? Retrieved from http://www.shunya.net/Text/Blog/DelhiCityOfRape.htm

Audit Bureau of Circulation. (2017). Retrieved April 2017 from http://www.auditbureau.org.

Bailey, A. & Chris, C. (2008). *The Feminist Philosophy Reader.* New York: McGraw-Hill.

Banerji, A. (2018, December 12). Where is the #MeToo moment in India's politics? Retrieved from https://in.reuters.com/article/india-politics-women/where-is-the-metoo-moment-in-indias-politics-idINKBN1OB1EF

References

Bangalore molestation: Police finds "credible evidence," registers FIR. (2017, January 4). *The Times of India*. Retrieved from https://timesofindia.indiatimes.com/india/bengaluru-moles tation-police-finds-credible-evidence-registers-fir/articleshow/56322593.cms

Baruah, P. (2012, December 20). Guwahati demands death penalty for rapists. *The Times of India*. Retrieved from https://timesofindia.indiatimes.com/city/guwahati/Guwahati-demands -death-penalty-for-rapists/articleshow/17685056.cms

Bastos, M. T., Raimundo, R.L.G., & Travitzki, R. (2013). Gatekeeping Twitter: Message diffusion in political hashtags. *Media, Culture and Society, 35*(2), 260–270. doi:10.1177 /0163443712467594

Basu, I. (October 30, 2016). 910 rape cases reported in Kerala in six months. Retrieved from https://www.huffingtonpost.in/2016/10/30/910-rape-cases-reported-in-kerala-in-six -months_a_21594810/

Beam, R. A., & Di Cicco, D. T. (2010). When women run the newsroom: Management change, gender, and the news. *Journalism & Mass Communication Quarterly, 87*(2), 393–411. https://doi.org/10.1177/107769901008700211

Bedi, Tarini (2006). Feminist theory and the right-wing: Shiv sena women mobilize Mumbai. *Journal of International Women's Studies, 7*(4), 51–68.

Bekkers, V., Beunders, H., Edwards, A., & Moody, R. (2011). New media, micromobilization, and political agenda setting: Crossover effects in political mobilization and media usage. *The Information Society, 27*(4), 209–219.

Belair-Gagnon, V., Mishra, S., & Agur, C. (2014). Reconstructing the Indian public sphere: Newswork and social media in the Delhi gang rape case. *Journalism, 15*(8), 1059–1075. doi:10.1177/1464884913513430

Belknap, J. (2010). Rape: Too hard to report and too easy to discredit victims. *Violence Against Women, 16*(12), 1335–1344. doi:10.1177/1077801210387749

Bhadra, K. & Chakrabarty, S. (July 18, 2013) Mamata Banerjee slams Kamduni rape protesters, gets angry send-off. *The Times of India*. Retrieved from https://timesofindia.indiatimes .com/india/Mamata-Banerjee-slams-Kamduni-rape-protesters-gets-angry-send-off /articleshow/20638913.cms

Bhandare, N. (2019, February 22). The long march to justice. *The Hindustan Times*. Retrieved from https://www.hindustantimes.com/columns/the-long-march-to-justice/story-F027 xHS8nRZxVQJ19zvtMO.html

Bhargavi, B., Guru, B., & Joseph, K. (2015, February). *Media scenario in India: An overview*. Retrieved from http://ijmsrr.com/downloads/280220157.pdf

Bhattacharya, A. (2017, March 13). "This is India's Uber": Sexual harassment allegations rattle India's top entertainment startup. Retrieved from http://qz.com/931134/this-is-indias -uber-sexual-harassment-allegations-rattle-indias-top-entertainment-startup-tvf/

Bhattacharya, A. (2019, September 13). #MeToo India: A year later, the men are back to work. What about the women? Retrieved from https://www.dailyo.in/voices/metoo-india -tanushree-dutta-metoo-movement-alok-nath-priya-ramani/story/1/32014.html

Bhattaccharyya, R. (2014). Understanding the spatialities of sexual assault against Indian women in India. In *Gender, Place & Culture: A Journal of Feminist Geography, 20*(9), 1340–1356.

Bianco, M. (2017, March 29). Nothing says misogyny like defining feminism as equality for all. Retrieved from https://qz.com/943068/the-future-of-feminism-the-gender-revolution -has-stalled-because-feminists-think-empowement-is-more-important-than-power/

Biswas, S. (2016, December 16). Hailing Nirbhaya as a martyr is unfair to her unjust death. Retrieved August 10, 2017, from http://indiatoday.intoday.in/story/nirbhaya-jyoti-singh -2012-delhi-gang-rape/1/836001.html

References

Blanding, M. (2018). Where does journalism end and activism begin? *Nieman Reports.* Retrieved from https://niemanreports.org/articles/where-does-journalism-end-and-activism-begin/

Bonnes, S. (2013). Gender and racial stereotyping in rape coverage. *Feminist Media Studies, 13*(2), 208–227. https://doi.org/10.1080/14680777.2011.623170

Borah, P. (2006, June). Brides are not for burning: A content analysis of newspaper coverage of dowry in India, 1999-2004. Paper presented at the annual meeting of the International Communication Association, Dresden, Germany

Boydstun, A. E. (2013). Making the news: politics, the media, and agenda setting.

BPO employee Prathibha Murthy case: Cab driver guilty, sentence on Friday. (2010, October 6). *NDTV.* Retrieved from https://www.ndtv.com/cities/bpo-employee-prathibha-murthy-case-cab-driver-guilty-sentence-on-friday-434549

Brimacombe, T., Kant, R., Finau, G., Tarai, J., & Titifanue, J. (2017). A new frontier in digital activism: An exploration of digital feminism in Fiji. *Asia & the Pacific Policy Studies.* Retrieved from https://doi.org/10.1002/app5.253.

Broadband Commission Working Group on Gender, UNESCO. (2015, September). *Cyber violence against women and girls.* Retrieved from https://en.unesco.org/sites/default/files/highlightdocumentenglish.pdf

Brooks, A. (2007). Feminist standpoint epistemology: Building knowledge and empowerment through women's lived experience. In Hesse-Biber, S. N., & Leavy, P. L. *Feminist research practice* (pp. 53–82). Thousand Oaks, CA: SAGE Publications, Inc. doi: 10.4135/9781412984270

Bruns, A. (2005). *Gatewatching: Collaborative online news production.* New York: P. Lang.

Bukhari, W. (2013). Awindra Pandey: Jyoti's death tortures me every single day. *The Sun.* Retrieved from https://www.thesun.co.uk/archives/news/451047/awindra-pandey-jyotis-death-tortures-me-every-single-day/

Casselman, B., Tankersley, J. & Smialek, J. (January 7, 2020). A year after a #MeToo reckoning, economists still grapple with it. *The New York Times.* Retrieved from https://www.nytimes.com/2020/01/07/business/economy/economics-race-gender.html

Cassidy, W. (2008). Outside influences: Extramedia forces and the newsworthiness conceptions of online newspaper journalists. First Monday, 13(1). doi:10.5210/fm.v13i1.2051

Carson, K. L. (2014, February). Big data mining and analytics. In *Encyclopedia of business analytics and optimization, 1,* (pp. 328–337).

Cassin, E. & Prasad, R. (November 6, 2017). Student's "sexual predator" list names professors. Retrieved from https://www.bbc.com/news/blogs-trending-41862615

Chadwick, A. (2013). The hybrid media system: Politics and power. New York: Oxford University Press.

Chadwick, A., & Smith, A. (2016). Politics in the age of hybrid media: Power, systems, and media logics. In A. Bruns, G. Enli, E. Skogerbø, A. O. Larsson, & C. Christensen (Eds.), *The Routledge companion to social media and politics* (pp. 7–22). New York: Routledge.

Chandola, A. (2018, October 24). #MeToo movement yet to reach rural India. Retrieved from https://www.villagesquare.in/2018/10/24/MeToo-movement-yet-to-reach-rural-india/

Changoiwala, P. (2019, September 24). How India fails its rape survivors. Retrieved from https://www.worldpoliticsreview.com/articles/28213/seven-years-after-nirbhaya-case-india-rape-victims-still-face-obstacles-to-justice

Chantler, K., & Gangoli, G. (2011). Domestic violence in minority communities: Cultural norm or cultural anomaly? In R. K. Thiara, S. Condon, & M. Schrottle (Eds.), *Violence against women and ethnicity: Commonalities and differences across Europe* (pp. 353–366). Berlin, Germany: Barbara Budrich Publishers.

References

Chattopadhyay, S. (2011) Online activism for a heterogeneous time: the pink chaddi campaign and the social media in India, *Proteus, 27*(1), 63–67.

Chaudhuri, M. (2000). "Feminism" in print media. *Indian Journal of Gender Studies, 7*(2), 263–288. doi:10.1177/097152150000700208

Chauhan, N., Ghosh, D., & Shekhar, R. (2012, December 18). Delhi gang rape case: Victim battles for life, 3 accused held. *The Times of India.* Retrieved from http://timesofindia .indiatimes.com/city/delhi/Delhi-gang-rape-case-Victim-battles-for-life-3-accused-held /articleshow/17656605.cms

Cheadle, H. (2017, January 6). How we can make social media less blindingly awful in 2017. Retrieved from http://www.vice.com/en_us/article/9abpkp/how-we-can-make-social -media-less-blindingly-awful-in-2017

Chopra, S. (2014). *The big connect: Politics in the age of social media.* New Delhi, India: Random Business.

Cole, E., & Daniel, J. H. (2005). *Featuring females: Feminist analyses of media.* Washington, DC: American Psychological Association.

Collins, P. (1998). It's all in the family: Intersections of gender, race, and nation. *Hypatia, 13*(3), 62–82. Retrieved July 22, 2020, from www.jstor.org/stable/3810699

Complaints of sexual harassment at workplace by women working in Judiciary. (2019, January 18). Retrieved from https://prsindia.org/content/complaints-sexual-harassment-work place-women-working-judiciary

Coulter, K., & Meyer, D. (2015). High profile rape trials and policy advocacy. *Journal of Public Policy, 35*(01), 35-61. doi:10.1017/S0143814X1400018X

Craft, S., & Wanta, W. (2004). Women in the newsroom: Influences of female editors and reporters on the news agenda. *Journalism & Mass Communication Quarterly, 81*(1), 124–138 . https://doi.org/10.1177/107769900408100109

Crenshaw, K. (1991). Mapping the margins: Intersectionality, identity politics, and violence against women of color. *Stanford Law Review, 43*(6), 1241–1299. Retrieved from doi:10.2307 /1229039

Crossley, A. D. (2015). Facebook feminism: Social media, blogs, and new technologies of contemporary U.S. feminism. *Mobilization: An International Quarterly, 20*(2), 253–268.

Cullen-Dupont, K (2009): Human Trafficking. New York: Infobase Publishing.

Danish. (2013, September 10). Delhi rape verdict: "Fast track court has set a precedent." Retrieved from http://www.firstpost.com/india/delhi-rape-verdict-fast-track-court-has -set-a-precedent-say-activists-1097889.html?utm_source=ref_article\

Dasgupta, P. (2018): "#MeToo in India: 75 professors, 30 institutes, what happened to Raya Sarkar's list of sexual harassers?" Retrieved from: https://www.huffingtonpost.in/2018/10 /25/metoo-in-india-75-professors-30-institutes-what-happened-to-raya-sarkar-s-list-of -sexual-harassers_a_23571422/

DeCapua, J. (2013, April 30). Better coverage of rape is needed. Retrieved from http://www .voanews.com/a/rape-media-30apr13/1651676.html

Delhi gang rape case: Cong women's wing rallies behind victim. (2012, December 21). *The Times of India.* Retrieved from https://timesofindia.indiatimes.com/city/bhubaneswar/Delhi -gang-rape-case-Cong-womens-wing-rallies-behind-victim/articleshow/17686898.cms?

Desai, S. (October 22, 2018). #MeToo as social regulation? *The Times of India.* Retrieved from https://timesofindia.indiatimes.com/blogs/Citycitybangbang/metoo-as-social -regulation/

Dey, A. (2016). A brief exploration of the effects of ICTs and social media on the gender activism in India post December 16th 2012. In C. Cerqueira; R. Cabecinhas & S. I. Magalhães (Eds.), *Gender in focus: (New) trends in media* (pp. 187–204). Braga, Portugal: CECS.

References 123

Dhanaraj, C. (November 18, 2018). MeToo and savarna feminism: Revolutions cannot start with the privileged, feminist future must be equal for all. Retrieved from https://www.firstpost.com/india/metoo-and-savarna-feminism-revolutions-cannot-start-with-the-privileged-feminist-future-must-be-equal-for-all-5534711.html

Dhawani, H. (2012, December 21). Parties cry foul, but field alleged rapists. *The Times of India*. Retrieved August 20, 2017, from http://timesofindia.indiatimes.com/india/Parties-cryfoul-but-field-alleged-rapists/articleshow/17700416.cms

Dhingra, S. (Oct. 21, 2018). Unnao teen has no clue of #MeToo, just wants her 'rapist' BJP MLA sacked. (2018). Retrieved from https://theprint.in/india/governance/unnao-teen-has-no-clue-of-metoo-just-wants-her-rapist-bjp-mla-sacked/137769/

DiBennardo, R. A. (2018). Ideal victims and monstrous offenders: how the news media represent sexual predators. *Socius: Sociological Research for a Dynamic World, 4*, 237802311880251–237802311880251. https://doi.org/10.1177/2378023118802512

Dreze, J., & Sen, A. (2013). *An uncertain glory: India and its contradictions.* Princeton, NJ: Princeton University Press.

D'Souza, R. (2009). NGOs in India's elite newspapers: A framing analysis. *Asian Journal of Communication, 20*(4), 477–493. doi:10.1080/01292986.2010.496863

Durham, M. G. (2013). Vicious assault shakes Texas town. *Journalism Studies, 14*(1), 1–12. doi: 10.1080/1461670X.2012.657907

Durham, M. G. (2015). Scene of the crime. *Feminist Media Studies, 15*(2), 175–191.

Dutt, S. (2019). "This is not an accident, it's a conspiracy." Retrieved from https://www.rediff.com/news/special/this-is-not-an-accident-its-a-conspiracy/20190730.htm

Dutta, D., & Sircar, O. (2013). India's winter of discontent: Some feminist dilemmas in the wake of a rape. *Feminist Studies, 39*(1), 293–306.

Eagle, R. B. (2015). Loitering, lingering, hashtagging: Women reclaiming public space via #BoardtheBus, #StopStreetHarassment, and the #EverydaySexism Project. *Feminist Media Studies, 15*(2), 350–353. doi:10.1080/14680777.2015.1008748

Eilders, C. (2001). *Conflict and consonance in media opinion: Political positions of five German quality papers.* Berlin: WZB Discussion Papers.

Elmore, C. (2007). Recollections in hindsight from women who left: the gendered newsroom culture. *Women and Language 30*(2): 18–27.

Erikson, A. (December 14, 2018). In 2018, #MeToo—and its backlash—went global. *The Washington Post.* Retrieved from https://www.washingtonpost.com/world/2018/12/14/metoo-its-backlash-went-global/

Everbach, T. (2006). The culture of a women-led newspaper: an ethnographic study of the Sarasota Herald-Tribune. *Journalism & Mass Communication Quarterly, 83*(3), 477–493. https://doi.org/10.1177/107769900608300301

Fadnis, D. (2017). Uncovering rape culture: Patriarchal values guide Indian media's rape-related reporting. *Journalism Studies, 19*(12), 1750–1766.

Flaherty, C. (2018). Why one academic spends hours a week putting together a spreadsheet of documented harassment cases, names and all. Retrieved from https://www.insidehighered.com/news/2018/09/20/why-one-academic-spends-hours-week-putting-together-spreadsheet-documented

Flaherty, C. (Oct. 17, 2017). Follow-up to study on misconduct at academic field sites says clear rules of conduct and enforcement are needed. Retrieved from https://www.insidehighered.com/news/2017/10/17/follow-study-misconduct-academic-field-sites-says-clear-rules-conduct-and

Fonow, M., & Cook, J. (2005). Feminist methodology: New applications in the academy and public policy. *Signs, 30*(4), 2211–2236. doi:10.1086/428417

References

4th acid attack on UP gang-rape survivor? (2017, July 3). *Lucknow News*. Retrieved August 20, 2017 from http://timesofindia.indiatimes.com/city/lucknow/4thacid-attack-on-up-gang-rape-survivor/articleshow/59416891.cms

Franiuk, R., Seefelt, J. L., Cepress, S. L., & Vandello, J. A. (2008). Prevalence and effects of rape myths in print journalism. *Violence Against Women, 14*(3), 287–309. doi: 10.1177/1077801207313971

Gajjala, R. (2019). *Digital diasporas: Labor, affect and technomediation in South Asia*. Lanham, MD: Lexington Press.

Gajjala, R. (September 2018).When an Indian Whisper Network Went Digital. In *Communication, Culture and Critique*, Volume 11 (3), pp 489–493, https://doi.org/10.1093/ccc/tcy025

Gallagher, M. (2007). Feminist media perspectives. In A. Valdivia, (Ed.), *A companion to media studies* (pp. 1–39). Malden, MA: Blackwell Publishing Ltd. doi:10.1002/9780470999066

Gamble, S. (2001): *The Routledge companion to feminism and postfeminism*. London: Routledge.

Gandhi, A. (2019). Tanushree's 'Closed' Case Will Fly Open Like a Stuffed Suitcase. Retrieved 20 July 2020, from https://www.thequint.com/neon/gender/tanushree-dutta-nana-patekar-closed-case

Gangoli, G., & Rew, M. (2014). "Strategic co-option"? Indian feminists, the state and legal activism on domestic violence. In N. Aghtaie and G. Gangoli (Eds.), *Understanding gender based violence: National and international contexts* (pp. 183–202). Abingdon, UK: Routledge.

Gangoli, G. (2011). *Indian feminisms: Law, patriarchies, and violence in India*. Hampshire, UK: Ashgate.

Gang-rape survivor attacked with acid in Lucknow. (2017, July 2). *The Times of India*. Retrieved from https://timesofindia.indiatimes.com/city/lucknow/acid-attack-victim-who-met-cm-yogi-adityanath-attacked-again/articleshow/59407317.cms

Gangrape survivor attacked with acid for fourth time in Lucknow. (2017, July 2). *The Indian Express*. Retrieved from https://indianexpress.com/article/india/uttar-pradesh-gang-rape-survivor-attacked-with-acid-for-third-time-in-lucknow-4731516/

Geertsema, M. (2009). Women and news: Making connections between the global and the local. *Feminist Media Studies, 9*(2), 149–172. doi:10.1080/14680770902814827

Ghonim, W. (2016, February 4). Let's design social media that drives real change [video file]. Retrieved from https://www.youtube.com/watch?v=HiwJohNl1Fw

Ghosh, D. (2012, December 23). I won't vanish without a fight, they will have to pay, Delhi gang-rape victim says. *The Times of India*. Retrieved from http://timesofindia.indiatimes.com/city/delhi/I-wont-vanish-without-a-fight-they-will-have-to-pay-Delhi-gang-rape-victim-says/articleshow/17725015.cms

Govt dissolves #MeToo panel quietly, refuses to divulge details: Report. (2019, July 22). Retrieved from https://thewire.in/government/metoo-group-of-ministers-posh-act

Groshek, J. (2008). Homogenous agendas, disparate frames: CNN and CNN International Coverage Online. *Journal of Broadcasting and Electronic Media, 52*(1), 52–68.

Guha, P. (2009, March 4). Only two women on LF poll list. *The Times of India*. Retrieved from https://timesofindia.indiatimes.com/city/kolkata/Only-two-women-on-LF-poll-list/articleshow/4220884.cms

Guha, P. (2015). Hash tagging but not trending: The success and failure of the news media to engage with online feminist activism in India. *Feminist Media Studies, 15*(1), 155–157. doi:10.1080/14680777.2015.987424

Guha, P. (2017). Mind the gap: Connecting news and information to build an anti-rape and sexual assault agenda in India. Retrieved from https://drum.lib.umd.edu/handle/1903/20743

References

Guha, R. (2015, January 3). Why women are so unsafe in our cities. *Hindustan Times*. Retrieved from http://www.hindustantimes.com/columns/why-women-are-so-unsafe-in-our-cities/story-8bcaMb7Xo2Iloa7130FabP.html

Gupta, S. (2018). #MetooIndia: My Chief Reporter Debdut Ghoshthakur sexually harassed me repeatedly, but Anandabazar Patrika did nothing. I was transferred instead. *The Bengal Story—English*. Retrieved from https://thebengalstory.com/english/metooindia-my-chief-reporter-debdut-ghoshthakur-sexually-harassed-me-repeatedly-but-anandabazar-patrika-did-nothing-i-was-transferred-instead/

Grzywiska, I. & Borden, J. (2012). The impact of social media on traditional media agenda settingtheory. The case study of Occupy Wall Street Movement in USA. In B. Dobek-Ostrowska, B. Lodzki, & W. Wanta (Eds.), *Agenda setting: Old and new problems in old and new media* (ss. 133–155). Wroclaw, Poland: University of Wroclaw Press.

"Had to stand up for Uber driver": Ex-Miss India on midnight horror in Kolkata. (2019, June 19). *NDTV*. Retrieved from https://www.ndtv.com/kolkata-news/kolkata-model-ushoshi-sengupta-chased-by-mob-went-to-police-told-not-our-jurisdiction-2055581

Hardin, M. & Shain, S. (2005). Strength in numbers? the experiences and attitudes of women in sports media careers. *Journalism & Mass Communication Quarterly*. Retrieved from https://journals.sagepub.com/doi/10.1177/107769900508200404

Harlow, S., & Harp, D. (2012). Collective action on the web: A cross-cultural study of social networking sites and online and offline activism in the United States and Latin America. *Information Communication and Society, 15*(2), 196–216. doi: 10.1080/1369118X.2011.591411

Harlow, S., & Guo, L. (2014). Will the revolution be tweeted or facebooked? using digital communication tools in immigrant activism. *Journal of Computer-Mediated Communication, 19*(3), 463–478. https://doi.org/10.1111/jcc4.12062

Harp, D. (2008). News, feminist theories, and the gender divide. In Poindexter, P. M., Meraz, S., & Weiss, A. S. (Eds.). *Women, men, and news: Divided and disconnected in the news media landscape.* New York: Routledge.

Hartsock, N. (2004). The feminist standpoint: developing the ground for a specifically feminist historical materialism, in Harding, Sandra (Ed.), *The feminist standpoint theory reader: Intellectual and political controversies.* New York: Routledge, pp. 35–54.

Hegde, R. (Ed.). (2011). *Circuits of visibility: Gender and transnational media cultures.* New York: New York University Press.

Hess, A. (2014, January 6). Why women aren't welcome on the internet. Retrieved from http://psmag.com/social-justice/women-arent-welcome-internet-72170

Hesse-Biber, S. (2010). Qualitative approaches to mixed methods practice. *Qualitative Inquiry, 16*(6), 455–468. https://doi.org/10.1177/1077800410364611

Himabindu, B. L., Arora, R., & Prashanth, N. S. (2014). Whose problem is it anyway? Crimes against women in India. *Global Health Action, 7*, 10.3402/gha.v7.23718. http://doi.org/10.3402/gha.v7.23718

Hirschauer, S. (2014). *The securitization of rape: Women, war and sexual violence.* New York: Palgrave Macmillan. https://doi.org/10.1057/9781137410825

Hollander, J. A., & Rodgers, K. (2014). Constructing victims: The erasure of women's resistance to sexual assault. *Sociological Forum, 29*(2), 342–364.

Holmgren, L. (2011). Cofielding in qualitative interviews: Gender, knowledge, and interaction in a study of (pro)feminist men. *Qualitative Inquiry, 17*(4), 364–378. doi:10.1177/1077800411401199

Housley, W. (2018). Conversation analysis, publics, practitioners and citizen social science. *Discourse Studies, 20*(3), 431–437. https://doi.org/10.1177/1461445618754581

References

Hyderabad rises against Delhi gang rape. (2012, December 23). *The Times of India*. Retrieved from https://timesofindia.indiatimes.com/city/hyderabad/Hyderabad-rises-against-Delhi-gang-rape/articleshow/17724646.cms

Iannelli, L. (2016). *Hybrid politics: Media and participation*. London: SAGE Publications.

IANS. (June 17, 2019). Former Miss India Universe chased and attacked in Kolkata, 7 held. Retrieved from https://www.outlookindia.com/newsscroll/former-miss-india-universe-chased-and-attacked-in-kolkata-7-held/1557525

Internet users in India to reach 627 million in 2019 (2019). Retrieved from https://economictimes.indiatimes.com/tech/internet/internet-users-in-india-to-reach-627-million-in-2019-report/articleshow/68288868.cms

Iosifidis, P. (2014). Social media, democracy and public service media. *Online Journal of Communication and Media Technologies, 4*, pp. 71–88.

Islam, A. (Aug, 6, 2016). Why acid attacks are on the rise in India. Retrieved from https://www.dw.com/en/why-acid-attacks-are-on-the-rise-in-india/a-19313750

Iyer, A. (2019). After RTI revealed #MeToo panel dissolved, govt reconstitutes GoM. Retrieved 20 July 2020, from https://www.thequint.com/voices/women/government-on-me-too-movement-rti-reveals-govt-dissolved-panel-stonewalls-queries

Jeffrey, R. (2000). *Capitalism, politics and the Indian-language press 1977–1999*. London: Hurst.

Jolly, J. (2016, July 20). Rape culture in India: The role of the English-language press. Retrieved from https://shorensteincenter.org/rape-culture-india-english-language-press/

Jones, A. (2016, October 31). Challenging slacktivism: Activism on social media is not enough. Retrieved from http://www.huffingtonpost.com/entry/challenging-slacktivism-activism-on-social-media_us_5817c2dbe4b09b190529c8ae

Joseph, A. (2008). Rape and the media. In S. Bhattacharjee (Ed.), *A unique crime: Understanding rape in India* (pp. 260–285). New Delhi, India: Oxford University Press.

Joseph, A. (2014). Action, reaction, introspection, rectification. In A. Viga Montiel, (Ed.), *Media and gender: A scholarly agenda for the global alliance on media and gender*. Paris, France: UNESCO.

Joyce, M. C. (2010). *Digital activism decoded: The new mechanics of change* (Preface, pp. 1–14). New York, NY: International Debate Education Association.

Justice Verma Committee Report Summary. (n.d.). Retrieved from https://www.prsindia.org/report-summaries/justice-verma-committee-report-summary

Kahn, R., & Kellner, D. (2012). Oppositional politics and the internet: A critical/reconstructive approach. In M. G. Durham & D. Kellner (Eds.), *Media and cultural studies: Keyworks* (pp. 598–625). Malden, MA: Wiley-Blackwell.

Kalkod, R. (2010). Know your rights: All about FIR. *The Times of India*. Retrieved from http://epaper.timesofindia.com

Kantor, J. & Twohey, M. (2019). *She said*. London: Penguin.

Kappal, B. (2017, November 30). Breaking the "savarna feminism" rules—how Raya Sarkar's list of alleged harassers divided opinion in India. *New Statesman*. Retrieved from https://www.newstatesman.com/politics/feminism/2017/11/breaking-savarna-feminism-rules-how-raya-sarkar-s-list-alleged-harassers

Kathua rape case: Top developments and reactions. (2018, April 14). *The Times of India*. Retrieved from https://timesofindia.indiatimes.com/india/kathua-rape-case-top-developments/articleshow/63762035.cms

Katzenstein, M. (1989). Organizing against violence: Strategies of the Indian women's movement. *Pacific Affairs, 62*(1), 53–71.

Kerala woman raped and killed, intestines ripped out in attack. (2016, May 2). *Hindustan Times*. Retrieved from http://www.hindustantimes.com/india/kerala-woman-raped-and-killed-intestines-ripped-out-in-attack/story moISHjg3F5vA7GUNRSg2nL.html

Khamis, S. (2010). Islamic feminism in new Arab media platforms for self-expression and sites for multiple resistances. *Journal of Arab & Muslim Media Research, 3*(3), 237–255.

Khan, F. L., & Pathak, S. (2019, July 29). India's #MeToo movement, one year on. Retrieved from https://www.npr.org/sections/goatsandsoda/2019/07/29/744444673/indias-metoo-movement-one-year-on

Khan, N. (2018, October 10). Raising my voice against sexual harassment made me lose my job at TOI. Retrieved from https://enewsroom.in/sexually-harassed-editor-toi-me-too/

Kilman, L. (2015a, February 12). Digital media India: Where print is king, digital is coming on strong. Retrieved from http://www.wan-ifra.org/press-releases/2015/02/12/digital-media-india-where-print-is-king-digital-is-coming-on-strong

Kilman, L. (2015b, June 1). World press trends: Newspaper revenues shift to new sources. Retrieved from https://www.wan-ifra.org/press-releases/2015/06/01/world-press-trends-newspaper-revenues-shift-to-new-sources

King, N. (1994). The qualitative research interview. In C. Cassell & G. Symon (Eds.), *Qualitative methods in organizational research: A practical guide* (pp. 14–36). London: SAGE.

Kolkata: Former Miss India Universe harassed by bike-borne youths, 7 held. (June 19, 2019). Economic Times. Retrieved from: https://economictimes.indiatimes.com/news/politics-and-nation/kolkata-former-miss-india-universe-harassed-by-bike-borne-youths-7-held/videoshow/69851701.cms?from=mdr

Krishnan, S. (2014). Responding to rape: Feminism and young middle-class women in India. In M. Alston (Ed.), *Women, political struggles and gender equality in South Asia* (pp. 19–32). New York: Palgrave Macmillan. doi:10.1057/9781137390578_2.

Kumar, R. (1993). *The history of doing: An illustrated account of movements for women's rights and feminism in India, 1800–1990*. London: Verso.

Lee, B., Lancendorfer, K., & Lee, K. J. (2005). Agenda setting and the internet: The intermedia influence of internet bulletin boards on newspaper coverage of the 2000 general election in South Korea. *Asian Journal of Communication, 15*(1), 57–71.

Lee, J. K. (2007). The effect of the internet on homogeneity of the media agenda: A test of the fragmentation thesis. *Journalism & Mass Communication Quarterly, 84*(4), 745–760.

Leurs, K. H. A. & Ponzanesi, S. (2014). Digital crossings in Europe. *Crossings: Journal of Migration & Culture, 5*(1), 1–181.

Lennon, S. (2013). Journalism, gender, feminist theory and news reporting on the Australian Football League. *Ejournalist, 13*(1), pp. 20–39. Retrieved from https://ejournalist.com.au/public_html/v13n1/Lennon.pdf

Losh, E. (2014). Hashtag feminism and Twitter activism in India. *Social Epistemology Review and Reply Collective, 3*(12), 10–22.

Lynes, K. G. (2012). A discrepant conjuncture: Feminist theorizing across media cultures. *Ada: A Journal of Gender, New Media, and Technology, 1*. doi:10.7264/N3H41PB4

Madhok, D. (2015, September 23). Sorry to break it to you, Priyanka Chopra, but you're a feminist. Retrieved from http://qz.com/509617/sorry-to-break-it-to-you-priyanka-chopra-but-youre-a-feminist/

Mahapatra, D. (October, 30, 2017). Naming, shaming through crowd sourcing is a double-edged weapon. Retrieved from https://times-of-india-new-delhi-edition/20171030/281981787845270

Mahr, K. (2013). Should the Indian gang-rape victim remain anonymous? *Time*. Retrieved from https://world.time.com/2013/01/04/should-the-indian-gang-rape-victim-remain-anonymous/

Majumdar, P. (2018, October 22). #Metoo: A supreme power called Ananda Bazar Patrika that guillotines women everyday. Retrieved from http://thebengalstory.com/english/metoo-a-supreme-power-called-ananda-bazar-patrika-that-guillotines-women-everyday/

128 References

Malvania, U. (2019, April 26). Print readership in India jumps 4.4% to 425 million in two years: Report. Retrieved from https://www.business-standard.com/article/current-affairs/print-readership-in-india-jumps-4-4-to-425-million-in-two-years-report-119042700079_1.html

Manjappa, S. V. (2014). *Impact of globalization on media management in India: An empirical study* (PhD thesis). University of Mysore, Karnataka, India.

Mantri, G. (2016, May 9). Media, law and patriarchy: Why Jisha's real name is more powerful than any pseudonym. Retrieved from http://www.thenewsminute.com/article/media-law-and-patriarchy-why-jishas-real-name-more-powerful-any-pseudonym-42861

Martin, M. & O'Carroll, T. (2019, January 6). Troll watch: Online harassment toward women [Audio recording]. In *All Things Considered*. Retrieved from https://www.npr.org/2019/01/06/682714973/troll-watch-online-harassment-toward-women

Martin, S. (2014). *Social media and participatory democracy: Public notice and the world wide web*. New York: Peter Lang.

Mass molestation that wasn't?. (January 15, 2017). *The Times of India*. Retrieved from https://timesofindia.indiatimes.com/home/sunday-times/the-mass-molestation-that-wasnt/articleshow/56557691.cms

McCombs, M. E. (2014). *Setting the agenda: The mass media and public opinion* (2nd ed.). Cambridge: Polity.

Mejias, U. A. (2013). *Off the network: Disrupting the digital world*. Minneapolis, MN: University of Minnesota Press.

Mendes, K. (2011). Reporting the women's movement. *Feminist Media Studies, 11*(4), 483–498. doi:10.1080/14680777.2011.555968

Mendoza, J. (2014, September 9). How media coverage of sexual violence gets it wrong. Retrieved from https://www.pri.org/stories/2014-09-09/how-media-coverage-sexual-violence-gets-it-wrong

Menon, M. (2019, September 18). "MeToo" and after. *Business Today*. Retrieved from https://www.businesstoday.in/magazine/columns/metoo-and-after/story/379290.html

Menon, N. (2017, October 24). Statement by feminists on Facebook campaign to "name and shame." Retrieved from https://kafila.online/2017/10/24/statement-by-feminists-on-facebook-campaign-to-name-and-shame/

Meraz, S. (2009). Is there an elite hold? Traditional media to social media agenda setting influence in Blog Networks. *JCC4 Journal of Computer-Mediated Communication, 14*(3), 682–707.

Meraz, S. (2011). The fight for "how to think": Traditional media, social networks, and issue interpretation. *Journalism, 12*(1), 107–127.

Messner, M., & Garrison, B. (2010). Sources without a name: An analysis of the source interaction between elite traditional news media and filter blogs. Retrieved from https://pdfs.semanticscholar.org/3494/8a54da5f4e860842024dbbc701e6a2eca829.pdf?_ga=2.268259406.1976835210.1583434465-1328740864.1583434465

Meyers, M. (1997). *News coverage of violence against women*. London: SAGE.

Meyers, M. (2004). African american women and violence: gender, race, and class in the news. *Critical Studies in Media Communication, 21*(2), 97–118.

Mihailidis, P. (2017, July 18). Civic media literacy. Lecture presented at Salzburg Global Media Academy in Austria, Salzburg.

Minh-ha, T. T. (Director). (1983). *Reassemblage: From the firelight to the screen*. [Documentary].

Minic, D. (2008). What makes an issue a woman's hour issue? *Feminist Media Studies, 8*(3), 301–315. doi:10.1080/14680770802217345

Mishra, S., Swaminathan, M., & Jayakumar, N. (2019, November 6). In conversation with Ammu Joseph: The #MeToo in media moment. Retrieved from https://feminisminindia.com/2019/11/06/ammu-joseph-metoo-media-moment/

Mitchell, A., & Holcomb, J. (2016, June 15). State of the news media 2016. Retrieved from https://www.journalism.org/2016/06/15/state-of-the-news-media-2016/2009/

Mitta, M. (2012, December 27). Rape fastest growing crime in the country. *The Times of India*. Retrieved from http://timesofindia.indiatimes.com/india/Rape-fastest-growing-crime -in-the-country/articleshow/17774115.cms

Mohanty, C. T. (2003). "Under Western Eyes" revisited: Feminist solidarity through anticapitalist struggles. *Signs: Journal of Women in Culture and Society, 28*(2), 251, 499–535. doi:10.1086/342914

More than 19,500 languages spoken in India: Census. (2018, July 1). *NDTV*. Retrieved from https://www.ndtv.com/india-news/more-than-19-500-languages-spoken-as-mother- tongue-in-india-census-1876085

Munro, E. (2013). Feminism: A fourth wave? *Political Insight, 4*(2), 22–25. doi:10.1111/ 2041-9066.12021

Nagar, I. (2016). Reporting rape: Language, neoliberalism, and the media. *Discourse and Communication, 10*(3), 257–273. doi:10.1177/1750481315623900

Nagar, R. (2010). Mujhe jawab do! (Answer me!): Women's grass-roots activism and social spaces in chitrakoot (India). *Gender, Place & Culture, 7*(4), 341–362. doi:10.1080/713668879

Nair, D. (2017, February 21). Sexual harassment—underbelly of the Indian startup ecosystem exposed. Retrieved from http://yourstory.com/2017/02/sexual-harassment-indian-startup -ecosystem/

Nandi, J. (2012, December 19). Angry students take to street, call for action. *The Times of India*. Retrieved from http://timesofindia.indiatimes.com/city/delhi/Angry-students-take-to -street-call-for-action/articleshow/17673058.cms

Narayan, U. (1997). *Dislocating cultures: Identities, traditions, and third world feminism*. New York: Routledge.

NCRB. (2017). Crime in India. Vol. 1. Retrieved from https://ncrb.gov.in/sites/default/files /Crime%20in%20India%202017%20-%20Volume%201_0.pdf

NCRB. (2019). Crime in India. Retrieved from https://ncrb.gov.in/en/crime-india-2018#

NDTV. (July 2, 2017). Fourth acid attack on Uttar Pradesh gang-rape survivor. She had full-time security. Retrieved from https://www.ndtv.com/india-news/uttar-pradesh-woman -gang-raped-9-years-ago-attacked-with-acid-for-third-time-1719433

Neighbour among 3 taken into custody for Kerala rape-murder. (2016, May 4). *Hindustan Times*. Retrieved from: https://www.hindustantimes.com/india/two-taken-into-custody -for-raping-and-killing-dalit-woman-in-kerala/story-IgZlaj5AmQqqRFlqI54amL.html

Neuman, R. W., Guggenheim, L., Mo Jang, S., & Bae, S. Y. (2014). The dynamics of public attention: Agenda-setting theory meets big data. *JCOM Journal of Communication, 64*(2), 193–214.

Neupane, S. (2014, September 1). Women's feature service: Mapping the struggles of feminism in India. Retrieved from http://www.passblue.com/2014/09/01/womens-feature -service-mapping-the-struggles-of-women-in-india/

Nguyen, A. & Western, M. (2006). "The complementary relationship between the Internet and traditional mass media: the case of online news and information." *Information Research, 11*(3) paper 259 [Available at http://InformationR.net/ir/11-3/paper259.html]

O'Hara, S. (2012). Monsters, playboys, virgins and whores: Rape myths in the news media's coverage of sexual violence. *Language and Literature, 21*(3), 247–259. https://doi.org/10 .1177/0963947012444217

Ohlheiser, A. (2018, January 22). How #MeToo really was different, according to data. Retrieved from https://www.washingtonpost.com/news/the-intersect/wp/2018/01/22 /how-metoo-really-was-different-according-to-data/

References

Otis, A. (2019). *Hicky's Bengal gazette.* Chennai, India: Westland

Pandey, G. (March, 17, 2017). The rape that led to India's sexual harassment law. Retrieved from https://www.bbc.com/news/world-asia-india-39265653

Pariser, E. (2011). *The filter bubble: What the internet is hiding from you.* New York: Penguin Press.

Patel, V., & Khajuria, R. (2016). *Political feminism in India.* Friedrich-Ebert-Stiftung. Retrieved from https://library.fes.de/pdf-files/bueros/indien/12706.pdf

Peterson, K. (2009). Revisiting downs' issue-attention cycle: International terrorism and U.S. public opinion. *Journal of Strategic Security, 2*(4), 1–16.

Phillips, M., Mostofian, F., Jetly, R., Puthukudy, N., Madden, K., & Bhandari, M. (2015). Media coverage of violence against women in India: A systematic study of a high-profile rape case. *BMC Women's Health, 15*(3), 1–10. doi:10.1186/s12905-015-0161-x

Poell, T., & Rajagopalan, S. (2015). Connecting activists and journalists. *Journalism Studies, 16*(5), 719–733. doi:10.1080/1461670X.2015.1054182

Prasanna, L. (2016, May 6). Justice delayed: Over 3,000 rape cases pending in state. *The Times of India.* Retrieved from http://timesofindia.indiatimes.com/city/thiruvananthapuram/Justice-delayed-Over-3000-rape-cases-pending-in-state/articleshow/52138776.cms

Pritam, A. (1977/2015). *The revenue ticket.* New Delhi: Times Books.

PTI. (2017, July 14). India now has highest number of Facebook users, beats US: Report. Retrieved from http://www.livemint.com/Consumer/CyEKdaltF64YycZsU720EK/Indians-largest-audience-country-for-Facebook-Report.html

PTI. (2018, October 12). Maneka Gandhi sets up panel to look into all MeToo cases. Retrieved from https://www.indiatoday.in/india/story/maneka-gandhi-metoo-movement-panel-1366760-2018-10-12

PTI. (2019, September 3). Woman commits suicide outside Haryana police station over inaction on her rape complaint. Retrieved from https://www.indiatoday.in/india/story/woman-suicide-haryana-police-inaction-her-rape-complaint-1595004-2019-09-03

Purkayastha, S. (March 2017). This should've been TVF's reply to charges against Arunabh Kumar. The Quint. Retrieved from https://www.thequint.com/news/india/this-shouldve-been-tvf-reply-to-molestation-charges-against-arunabh-kumar

Ragas, M. W. (2014). Intermedia agenda setting in business news coverage. In R. Hart (Ed.), *Communication and language analysis in the public sphere* (pp. 335–357). Hershey, PA: IGI Global.

Rakow, L. (2012). Feminist theory. In P. Moy (Ed.), *Communication.* New York: Oxford University Press. doi:10.1093/obo/9780199756841-0093

Ram, N. (2016, February 29). Holding the newspaper to account. *The Hindu.* Retrieved from http://www.thehindu.com/opinion/op-ed/nram-on-holding-the-newspaper-to-account/article8292583.ece

Rana, P. (2014, February 12). India among the Worst for Press Freedom. *The Wall Street Journal.* Retrieved from http://blogs.wsj.com/indiarealtime/2014/02/12/india-among-the-worlds-worst-for-press-freedom/

Rao, S. (2014). Covering rape in shame culture: Studying journalism ethics in India's new television news media. *Journal of Mass Media Ethics, 29*(3), 153–167.

Rashid, O. (2019, December 9). Love, betrayal and caste oppression in an Unnao village. Retrieved from https://www.thehindu.com/news/national/other-states/unnao-rape-victim/article30236853.ece

Ray, R. (1999). *Fields of protest: Women's movements in India.* Minneapolis, MN: University of Minnesota Press.

Roberts, M., & McCombs, M. (1994). Agenda setting and political advertising: Origins of the news agenda. *Political Communication, 11*(3), 249–262. doi:10.1080/10584609.1994.9963030

Robin, J. (2000) *India's newspaper revolution: Capitalism, politics and the Indian-language press, 1977–1999.* New York: St. Martin's Press.

Rodriguez, R., & Ofori, K. (2001). Reinventing minority media for the 21st century. Retrieved from https://assets.aspeninstitute.org/content/uploads/files/content/docs/cands/DIVERSITY.PDF

Rodrigues, U. & Ranganathan M. 2015. *Indian news media: From observer to participant.* New Delhi: SAGE Publications.

Ross, K., & Carter, C. (2011). Women and news: A long and winding road. *Media, Culture & Society, 33*(8), 1148–1165. https://doi.org/10.1177/0163443711418272

Roy, S. (2015). The Indian women's movement: Within and beyond the NGOisation paradigm. *Journal of South Asian Development, 10*(1), 96–117.

Roy, S. (November 1, 2017). Whose feminism is it anyway? *The Wire.* Retrieved from https://thewire.in/gender/whose-feminism-anyway

Russell, A. (2016). *Journalism as activism: Recoding media power.* Cambridge: Polity Press.

Sayre, B., Bode, L., Shah, D., Wilcox, D., & Shah, C. (2010). Agenda setting in a digital age: Tracking attention to California Proposition 8 in social media, online news and conventional news. *Policy & Internet, 2*(2), 7–32.

Scharff, C., Smith-Prei, C., & Stehle, M. (2016). Digital feminisms: Transnational activism in German protest cultures. *Feminist Media Studies, 16*(1), 1–16. doi:10.1080/14680777.2015.1093069

Schrøder, K. (2015) News media old and new. *Journalism Studies, 16*(1), 60–78. doi: 10.1080/1461670X.2014.890332

Schulte, S. (2011). Surfing feminism's online wave: The internet and the future of feminism. *Feminist Studies, 37*(3), 727–744. Retrieved from www.jstor.org/stable/23069943

Schuster, J. (2013). Invisible feminists? Social media and young women's political participation. *Political Science, 65*(1), 8–24. doi:10.1177/0032318713486474

Sengupta, S. (2006). I/me/mine—intersectional identities as negotiated minefields. *Signs, 31*(3), 629–639.

Shah, A. H. (2018). How episodic frames gave way to thematic frames over time: A topic modeling study of the Indian media's reporting of rape post the 2012 Delhi gang-rape. *Poetics, 72,* 54–69. doi:10.1016/j.poetic.2018.12.001

Shenomics. (2016, December 15). 5 uninformed ideas that make feminism a bad word in India. Retrieved from http://www.huffingtonpost.in/shenomics/5-uninformed-ideas-that-make-feminism-a-bad-word-in-india_a_21628411/

Shome, R. (2006). Transnational feminism and communication studies. *The Communication Review, 9*(4), 255–267.

Sikanku, G. (2011). Intermedia influences among Ghanaian online and print news media: Explicating salience transfer of media agendas. *Journal of Black Studies, 42,* 1320–1335. doi:10.1177/0021934711417435.

Silver, B. (1988). Periphrasis, power, and rape in "A Passage to India." *Novel: A Forum on Fiction, 22*(1), 86–105.

Singer, J. (2014). User-generated visibility: Secondary gatekeeping in a shared media space. *New Media and Society, 16*(1), 55–73. doi:10.1177/1461444813477833

Singh, A. (2016, May 9). BJP ups ante in Kerala rape case, throws CBI probe poser at Congress. *The Times of India.* Retrieved from https://timesofindia.indiatimes.com/india/BJP-ups-ante-in-Kerala-rape-case-throws-CBI-probe-poser-at-Congress/articleshow/52170681.cms

132 References

Social justice minister raises questions on probe into Kerala rape and murder. (May 11, 2016). *Hindustan Times*. Retrieved from https://www.hindustantimes.com/india/social-justice-minister-raises-questions-on-probe-into-kerala-rape-and-murder/story-YJJNkqGoIK5czBeJlpCKmI.html

The Society for the Study of Artificial Intelligence and Simulation of Behaviour. (2014, September 5). What is AI? Retrieved from http://www.aisb.org.uk/public-engagement/what-is-ai

Spivak, G. (1999). *A critique of postcolonial reason: Toward a history of the vanishing present.* Cambridge, MA: Harvard University Press.

Statista. (2019, November 13). Newspaper industry in India. Retrieved from https://www.statista.com/topics/4726/newspaper-industry-in-india/

Steeves, H. (1987). Feminist theories and media studies. *Critical Studies in Mass Communication, 4*(2), 95–135. doi:10.1080/15295038709360121

Steeves, H. (2001). Liberation, feminism, and development communication. *Communication Theory, 11*(4), 397-414. doi: 10.1111/j.1468-2885.2001.tb00250.x

Steiner, L. (2013). Less falseness as antidote to the anxieties of postmodernism. In B. Brennen (Ed.), *Assessing evidence in a postmodern world* (pp. 113–136). Milwaukee, WI: Marquette University Press.

Sushmita. (2018, October 22). As #MeToo mounts, Bhanwari Devi's struggle must not be forgotten. Retrieved from https://indianculturalforum.in/2018/10/22/as-metoo-mounts-bhanwari-devis-struggle-must-not-be-forgotten/

Tarlo, E. (2001). *Unsettling memories: narratives of the emergency in Delhi.* Berkeley: University of California Press.

Thakuri, P. (2017, June 24). 5 years on, it's the same ordeal for Nirbhayas. *The Times of India*. Retrieved from https://timesofindia.indiatimes.com/city/delhi/5-years-on-its-the-same-ordeal-for-nirbhayas/articleshow/59292556.cms

Thayer, M. (2001). Transnational feminism: Reading Joan Scott in the Brazilian Sertao. *Ethnography, 2*(2), 243–271.

Thomas, R. G. C. (2006). Media. In S. Wolpert (Ed.), *Encyclopaedia of India* (Vol. 3, pp. 105–107). Farmington Hills, MI: Thomson Gale.

Thornham, S. (2001). *Feminist theory and cultural studies: Stories of unsettled relations.* London: Arnold.

Treré, E. (2018). *Hybrid media activism: Ecologies, imaginaries, algorithms.* London: Routledge.

University Grants Commission (UGC). (2013). UGC regulations. Retrieved from https://www.ugc.ac.in/page/ugc-regulations.aspx

Unnao rape survivor critical, on life support system: AIIMS sources. (2019, August 6). *The Times of India*. Retrieved from https://timesofindia.indiatimes.com/india/unnao-rape-survivor-critical-on-life-support-system-aiims-senior-doctor/articleshow/70551256.cms

Unnao rape victim alleges confinement; accused MLA's wife seeks narco test. (2018, April 11). Retrieved from https://www.rediff.com/news/report/confined-to-hotel-room-no-water-teen-in-unnao-rape-controversy/20180411.htm

Van Zoonen, L. (1994). *Feminist media studies.* Thousand Oaks, CA: SAGE.

Vatuk, S (2008). Islamic feminism in India? Indian Muslim women activists and the reform of Muslim person law. In F. Osella and C. Osella, eds., *Islamic Reform in India,* special issue, *Modern Asian Studies, 42* (2 & 3): 489–518.

Velayanikal, M. (2016, September 6). The latest numbers on web, mobile, and social media in India. Retrieved from http://www.techinasia.com/india-web-mobile-data-series-2016

Verma, S. (2016, May 3). For women, TN safer than educated Kerala. *The Times of India*, New Delhi edition. Retrieved from http://epaperbeta.timesofindia.com/Article.aspx?eid

=31808&articlexml=DATA-VISION-For-women-TN-safer-than-educated-030520
16014029

Virmani, P. (2016, July 6). Why is the rape crisis in rural India passing under the radar? *The Guardian.* Retrieved from https://www.theguardian.com/global-development/2016/jul/06/why-is-the-crisis-in-rural-india-passing-under-the-radar

Vitak, J., Shilton, K., & Ashktorab, Z.(2016). Beyond the Belmont Principles: Ethical challenges, practices, and beliefs in the online data research community. In *Proceedings of the 19th ACM Conference on Computer Supported Cooperative Work and Social Computing.* New York, NY: ACM.

Vyas, S. (2005, December 30). Shootout has no impact on city BPO staff. *The Times of India.* Retrieved June 16, 2016.

Walgrave, S., & Van Aelst, P. (2006). The contingency of the mass media's political agenda setting power: Toward a preliminary theory. *Journal of Communication, 56*(1), 88–109.

Weinbaum, A., Thomas, L., Ramamurthy, P., Poiger, U., Dong, M., & Barlow, T. (Eds.). (2008). *The modern girl around the world: Consumption, modernity, and globalization.* Durham: Duke University Press. doi:10.2307/j.ctv11hpjj4

West, L. (Feb, 1, 2018): I quit Twitter and it feels great. Retrieved from https://www.nytimes.com/2018/02/01/opinion/quitting-twitter-lindy-west.html

Wilhelm, H. (2019, May 31). Where #MeToo goes off the rails. Retrieved from https://www.chicagotribune.com/opinion/commentary/ct-perspec-me-too-sexual-assault-wilhelm-1023-story.html

Willnat, L., Weaver, D. & Wilhoit, G. (2017). The American journalist in the digital age: How journalists and the public think about journalism in the United States. *Journalism Studies, 20*(3): 423–441. https://doi.org/10.1080/1461670X.2017.1387071

Winfrey, O. (2014). *What I know for sure.* New York: Flatiron Books.

Women molested on New Year eve, minister blames 'western ways'. (January 2, 2017). Retrieved from https://economictimes.indiatimes.com/news/politics-and-nation/women-molested-on-new-year-eve-minister-blames-western-ways/articleshow/56296847.cms

Worthington, N. (2008). Encoding and decoding rape news: How progressive reporting inverts textual orientations. *Women's Studies in Communication, 31*(3), 344–367.

Worthington, N. (2013). Explaining gang rape in a "rough town": Diverse voices in gender violence news online. *Communication, Culture & Critique, 6*(1), 103–120. doi:10.1111/j.1753-9137.2012.01145.x

Wu, S., Hoffman, J., Winter, M., & Watts, D. (2011). Who says what to whom on Twitter. In *International World Wide Web Conference Committee (IW3C2) (ed) WWW 2011.* Hyderabad, India. Available at: http://www.wwwconference.org/proceedings/www2011/proceedings/p705.pdf

Yamaguchi, T. (2014). "Gender free" Feminism in Japan: A story of mainstreaming and backlash. *Feminist Studies, 40*(3), 541–572. Retrieved July 22, 2020, from www.jstor.org/stable/10.15767/feministstudies.40.3.541

Yu, S. (2009). Third-wave feminism: A transnational perspective. *Asian Journal of Women's Studies, 15*(1), 7–25.

Zeldin, W. (2013, April 9). Global legal monitor. Retrieved from https://www.loc.gov/law/foreign-news/article/india-criminal-law-amendment-bill-on-rape-adopted/

INDEX

Note: Page numbers in *italics* denote figures.

abnormality of perpetrators, as myth frame, 37
abuse, sexual: fear of, 1; sharing of, on social
  media, 92, 103; in the workplace, 90–91,
  111–113
academia, 23, 58, 70–73. *See also* #LoSHA
accountability of news media, 36
acid attacks, 46–47, 95–96
action/inaction: and agenda-building, 43,
  101–104, 106–108, 112; hashtag movements in,
  85, 88–89, 95–96, 98–99, 100–101; selective
  outrage in, 48
Adam, Karla, 66–67
affinity groups, Facebook, 91–92
agency, 64, 99–100, 101–102, 109–110, 111
agenda-building/setting: celebrity in, 107–108;
  dependence on news media in, 64, 81–94;
  framing of rape in, 24–25, 42–45, *43*; in
  hashtag movements, 61–62, 64–68; interdependent, 43, 44–45, 101–111, 112; intermedia, 59–62; journalists in, 24–25, 42–45,
  103–106, 112–113; in news coverage, 93;
  social media networks in, 61, 62–66, 77
agendamelding, 108–109
Akbar, M. J., 90, 111–112
Alat, Z., 15–16, 37, 39
algorithms, 54, 100–101
Althaus, S. L., 60
Alva, Nivedith, 98
Amit, journalist, 50
amplification of stories, 4, 25, 49–50, 95–96, 111
analysis, network, 68–69, *69*, 70, 73, *73*–81, *74*
Ananda Bazar Patrika, 103
Andelsman, V.: "If It Bleeds It Leads," 48
Andrews, K., 64–65
anonymity, 11, 82, 106–107
Arab Spring, 64–65
Ardovini-Brooker, J., 36
Asifa, rape of, 86–87, 88, 112
audience: in agenda-building, 24–25, 43, 45,
  108–110; in feminist media theories, 28–29,
  32–33; in framing via Facebook, 47–48; in

hashtag movements, 60, 62–63, 68, 90, 94–95;
  and rape myths, 36, 38
awareness/awareness raising: in agenda-
  building and setting, 65, 77, 92–93, 94, 101–102,
  110; in framing of rape, 15, 43–44; gap
  with action and agency, 99–100, 101–102,
  111; newspaper coverage in, 112; of online
  monitoring, 11–12; and selective outrage,
  48, 49–50; of social media's impact on
  policy, 92

backlash, 23, 41, 42, 50, 66, 70–73, 112
Bae, S. Y., 62–63
Bailey, A., 27
balance in framing of rape, 18, 38
Baruah, Pranjal, 52
Bates, Laura, 66–67
Beam, R. A., 31
Bee, Rameeza, 3
Bekkers, V., 108–109
Bengal, rural, 50
Bengal Story, The, 103–104
Beunders, H., 108–109
Bhattacharyya, A., 111–112
biases, 8, 14, 15, 18–19, 32–33, 51. *See also* outrage,
  selective
Biswas, Shiuli, 103
#BlackLivesMatter, 34, 61, 65
Black Twitter, 34
bloggers/blogging, 59, 60–61, 64–66, 106–107,
  108–109
Bollywood/Bollywoodization, 88, 89, 111–112
Booth, William, 66–67
Borden, J., 64–66
Boydstun, A. E., 63, 66
Breakthrough India, 73, *74*, 75–77, *77*
Brooks, A., 31
brutality: in depth of coverage, 48–49, 93; of
  Jisha's rape and murder, 85; of Jyoti Singh's
  gang-rape and murder, 5–6, 25, 37–38, 81,
  83–84; by police, 34, 61

135

136   Index

Caren, N., 64–65
Caringella-MacDonald, S., 36
Carter, C., 29
cascading model of top-down information, 65–66
cascading network activation, 65–66
caste: in agenda building, 25; in hashtag movements, 71–72, 79–80; in identification of victims by the press, 82–83, 94; in the Indian feminist movement, 14; in selective outrage, 49–50, 85
celebrities/celebrity, 23–24, 37, 72, 88, 89, 92–93, 107–108
censorship, 35–36, 40
Cepress, S. L., 37
Chandola, A., 53
charges filed, 57–58, 101, 101–102, 111
Cheadle, Harry, 99
Chinmay, blogger and journalist, 47–48, 87, 94–95
Chris, C., 27
class, socioeconomic, 17–18, 25, 37, 50, 79–80
CNN/CNN International Online, 60–61
commentary on social media pages, 76–77, 78, 78–81, 81
commodification of news and media, 14–15, 35–36, 110–111
communications, digital, 2–3
comparison, connective, 41
complaints, official, 49–50, 57–58, 89, 94, 97–98, 101–103, 107–108
connections/connected pages, social media, 75–76, 77–78, 79–80
"consent" of the victim, 15–16
conversation: in agenda-building/setting, 43, 65–66; as feminist research method, 7
Converse-McGuire Model, 65–66
convictions, 5–6, 57–58, 101, 101–102
Crenshaw, K., 33, 36–37
Criminal Law of 2013, 85, 94
cultural feminism, 31
culture, 17–19, 28, 83, 90
cyberfeminism, 30–31, 35, 68–69
cyberharassment, 2–3
cybervigilantism, 43–44

Dalit feminist platforms, 72
Dalit women, 14–15, 49–50, 53, 54, 57, 79, 80, 85. See also caste; Jisha, rape and murder of

datafication of hashtag movements, 89
Debamoy, journalist, 48, 50, 56–57
dehumanization of victims, 82
Delhi, 51–53, 99–100
Delhi gang-rape case of 2012. See Singh, Jyoti, gang-rape and murder of
demographics of social media users, 11
dependence/interdependence of news and social media, 42–45, 43, 56, 64, 81–94, 101–111, 112–113
Desai, S., 25
Devi, Bhanwari, 3–4
Dey, Adrija, journalist and activist, 43, 56
Dhanaraj, Christina, 14–15, 48
DiBennardo, R. A., 17
dichotomies in framing of rape, 15–16, 35–40
Di Cicco, D. T., 31
Diganta, journalist, 48–49, 56
discourse analysis, 40–42
discrimination, 5, 14, 28, 44–45, 87–88. See also outrage, selective
diversity, 8, 13–14, 29–30, 61–62, 66
divide, digital, 19, 24–25, 44, 54–55, 89. See also literacy, digital
Divya, activist, 49
doubting of victims, 19–20, 90, 106–107
Dreze, J., 40
due diligence, 57–58
due process, 23, 101–103
Durham, M. G., 15, 35
Dutta, D., 43–44
Dutta, Tanushree, 98
Dyuti, activist, 46–47

Eagle, R. B., 43
editors, 38–39, 48, 50, 55, 59–60
Edwards, A., 108–109
election campaigns, 24, 56, 61–62, 93–94, 96, 109
Elmore, C., 39
engagement, public: in agenda-building, 42–43, 45, 111; and selective outrage, 47; in sexual assault discourse, 41–42; in transnational hashtag movements, 74, 78–81, 81, 84, 85, 90–91, 91, 111, 112
entertainment industry, 103, 111–112
epistemology, feminist, 30–32
equality in feminism, 6–7, 26–27, 28
ethics, 10–12, 14–15, 31, 35–36, 68

ethnography in newsroom sexual assault discourse, 40–41
experience, personal, 31–32, 33–34, 46–47, 55
exploitation, 11, 38–39

Facebook: in agenda-building/setting, 68–69, 70–71, 73–75, 78–81, *81*, 90–92, *91*, 106–108; in agenda-setting, 106–108; anti-harassment campaigns on, 24; concerns of activists about, 99; ethical challenges in data collection from, 11–12; in rural activism, 45; users' influence on framing of rape and sexual assault, 47–48
Facebook messenger, 45
feminism/feminist movements: agenda-building in, 66–68; antirape, learning from, 97–113; "feminism without borders," 6–7; feminist media theories, 26–35, 42; in gatekeeping, 54; grassroots, 13, 14, 19–20, 42–45, *43*, 49–50, 89, 92; heterogeneity of, 13–14; on #LoSHA, 23, 70–72; in the media landscape, 2–3, 4; rape script approach in, 26–40; schools of, 29–31; stigmatization of, 5
Feminism in India (FII), 73, *73*, 77–80, *78*
feminist standpoint epistemology (FSE), 31–32
feminist Twitter, 34
filter bubble problem, 99, 100–101, 110
first-wave feminism, 27
follow-up by media and authorities, 48–49, 51, 52, 58, 86
fourth-wave feminism, 27
framing of rape in the news media: agenda-building in, 24–25, 42–45, *43*; feminist theorization on, 26–35; gender in, 16–17, 36–37, 38–40, 41–42; intersectionality in, 19–20, 25, 35–37, 39–40, 50; location in, 51; mythology in, 15–17, 34, 35–40; newsrooms in, 14–15, 29, 35–36, 38–42; politicization and politics in, 14–15, 17–19, 35–36, 41, 93–94, 96; rape culture in, 90; and selective outrage, 47–48, 50, 51; sexual assault discourse in, 40–42
Franiuk, R., 37

Gajjala, R., 71, 72
Gallagher, M., 15, 42
#GamerGate, 34

Gandhi, Maneka, 4
Gangoli, G., 19, 26
gang-rapes: framing of, 17–18, 25, 37–38, 43–44; in the media landscape, 3–4, 5–6; ongoing challenges for victims of, 99–100; as political issue, 56; in transnational hashtag movements, 81, 83–85, 88, 95–96. See also under *name of victim*; rapes
gatekeeping: in agenda-building, 24–25, 43, 44–45, 65–66, 108–110; by news media, 5–6, 54, 104–105; NGOs and nonprofits in, 9, 50; in rural activism, 95; in selective outrage, 54–55, 72–73; on social media networks, 70
Geertsema, M., 39–40
gender: as communicative process, 30; in feminist theorization on the media, 29, 32–33; in framing of rape, 16–17, 36–37, 38–40, 41–42; in framing of women by Facebook pages, 81; in intertwining of journalism and activism, 55; in the newsroom, 29, 38–40, 41–42; in second-wave feminism, 27; in undercoverage of rape, 50
"gender free" approach to discourse, 41
Ghonim, Wael, 97, 99
Ghosh, Dwaipayan, 26, 52
Ghoshthakur, Debdut, 103–104, 105
Global South, 18–19, 27–28, 31, 32, 39–40
Google, 66, 67–68, *67–68*, 70
Groshek, J., 60–61
Grzywiska, I., 64–66
Guggenheim, L., 62–63
Guo, L., 100–101
Gupta, Saberee, 103–105
Gyanesh, journalist, 47–48, 51, 56–57

harassment, online, 98–99
Harlow, S., 54–55, 100–101
Harp, D., 28–29, 54–55
hashtag movements, transnational: in agenda-building and setting, 61–62, 64–68; in awareness-raising, 43–44; background of, 83–94; internet mapping of, 68–69, *69*; learning from, 97–99; network analysis of, 73–81; politics and backlash against, 70–73; restrictions on, 54
He for She campaign, 65
Hegde, R., 16, 18, 37–38

138 Index

hegemony in framing of rape, 15, 32, 34–36, 39
heterogeneity. *See* diversity
Hickey's Bengal Gazette, 20
hierarchy: in feminist collaboration, 7; in
   framing of rape, 26, 35–36, 41; in hashtag
   movements, 90; in Indian nonprofits, 44–45;
   in NGOs and nonprofits, 9, 50; in selective
   outrage, 51, 54–55
#HimToo, 90
Hindustan Times, 53, 53–54
Hitendra, journalist, 96
#Hollaback!/#HollabackMumbai!, 68–69, 69
Hollander, J. A., 14–15, 16–17, 35–36, 40–41
honor of victims and their families, 5–6, 18,
   26, 37–38

#IamCharlie, 61
Ianelli, Laura: *Hybrid Politics: Media and
   Participation,* 19
identification of victims, 10, 82–83, 94
identity, sociocultural, 13, 19–20, 33, 37, 50, 80,
   93, 98–99
ideology, 8–9, 13, 15, 27, 28–29, 34–35
inclusivity: in agenda-building/setting,
   44–45, 63–64, 68; in discourse of rape and
   sexual harassment, 4; in framing of rape,
   24, 39–40, 42, 44–45; in hashtag movements,
   69, 72–73, 89; internet access in, 113; in
   research methods, 6–7
"India Fowler," 106–107
Indian Evidence Act, 85
Indian Penal Code, 82
information: in agenda-building, 100–101;
   cascading model of, 65–66; flow of, in
   agenda-building, 109–110; misinformation,
   37, 55, 100–101; reverse flow of, in
   agenda-setting, 62–63
informed consent, 12
infrastructure, urban, 51–53
intentionality of users, 12
interaction, feminist ideal of, 6–7
interdependence. *See* dependence/
   interdependence of news and social media
internet: access to, 19–20, 87, 89, 113; in agenda
   setting and building, 60–61; in fourth-wave
   feminism, 27; local factors in activism on,
   19–20; mapping of hashtag movements on,
   68–69, 69; in the media landscape, 2–3
Internet Researchers, Association of (AoIR),
   11–12

intersectionality: in commentary on Facebook
   pages, 79–80; in feminist theorization on
   the media, 31, 32–34, 35, 42; in framing of
   rape, 19–20, 25, 35–37, 39–40, 50; in the rape
   script approach, 26; in research methods,
   6–7; and selective outrage, 50, 54. *See also*
   marginalization/marginalized groups
Islamic feminism, 35
#IWillRideWithYou, 61
Iyer, A., 97–98

Jisha, rape and murder of, 52–53, 54, 56, 74–75,
   76–83, 85, 92–94, 93, 101–102
#Jisha, 90–91, 91
Jones, Amanda, 99
Joseph, Ammu, 14–15, 21–22, 35, 40–41
journalism/journalists: and activists, 55–58;
   in agenda-building and setting, 24–25,
   42–45, 62–63, 103–106, 112–113; digital, 21;
   in feminist media theories, 28–29; as focus
   of #MeToo campaigns, 23–24; in framing
   of rape, 18–19, 39–45, 47–48; FSE in, 31; in
   hashtag movements, 92; in recruitment of
   activist interviewees, 9–10; sexual
   harassment allegations by, 104–106, 111–112
justice: in agenda-building/setting, 70, 84–85,
   86, 87, 88, 90–91, 101, 106; obstacles to, 57
Justice Verma Commission, 4, 84–85, 94, 99–100

Kahn, R., 34
Kamduni gang-rape case, 42, 56
Kantor, J., 111
Katzenstein, M., 13–14
Kavita, journalist and activist, 55
Kellner, D., 34
Kelsky, Karen, 70
Khamis, S., 35
Khan, Nasreen, 105–106
Krishnan, S., 26
Kumar, Arunabh, 106–107
Kumar, R., 13–14

Lancendorfer, K., 59–61
language, 8, 15, 16–17, 90
law, Indian, 3–4, 10, 82, 85, 94, 99–100. *See also*
   policy, public
law enforcement, 19, 26, 88–89, 94, 95–96,
   101–103, 107–108. *See also* police
Lee, B., 59–61, 62
Lee, J., 64–65, 109

Lee, K. J., 59–61
Lennon, S., 30–31
LGBTQ community, 14
liberal feminism, 29–31
literacy, digital, 12, 24–25, 44, 87, 89, 111. *See also* divide, digital
location, 25, 49–54, 71, 79–80, 92. *See also* rural/urban divide
Losh, E., 43–44
#LoSHA (list of sexual harassers in academia), 23–24, 54, 66, 70–72
Lynes, K. G., 6

Madhya Pradesh, 51–52
Majumdar, Pallavi, 103–105
male-centricity in sexual assault news, 5–6, 18, 37–38
Malik, Anu, 90
Mantri, Geetika, 85
marginalization/marginalized groups: in feminist theorization on the media, 31–34; in framing of rape, 14–15, 16, 19–20, 31–32; in hashtag movements, 70, 71, 72–73, 87, 89, 90–91, 92, 95; selective outrage in activism for, 54; in transnational feminism and digital activism, 33–34. *See also* intersectionality
Marxist-socialist feminist theory, 29–31, 35–36
mass rape, 40. *See also* gang-rapes
Mathura gang-rape case, 3, 85, 118n4
McCombs, M. E., 59–60, 62–64, 108–109
media landscape, 2–6
media studies, feminist theories in, 28–33
Mendoza, J., 15
Menon, Meenakshi, 112
Meraz, S., 108–109
#MeToo and #MeTooIndia: in agenda-building, 24–25, 42–45; in feminist theorizing of media, 26–35; learning from, 111–112; in the media landscape, 2–4; politics and backlash in, 70–73; selective outrage in, 46–47, 49–50, 53–54, 55–58. *See also* hashtag movements, transnational
#MeTooRising, 67–68, 67–68
Minh-ha, Trinh T.: *Reassemblage,* 97
minorities/minority communities. *See* marginalization/marginalized groups
misogyny, 15, 27
Mitchelstein, E.: "If It Bleeds It Leads," 48
mobilization, meso- and micro-, 108–109
Mo Jang, S., 62–63

monetization of social media posts, 110–111
Moody, R., 108–109
morality, 16–17, 26–27, 36, 102–103
Morgan, Robin, 39–40
movements, oppositional, 90
Ms. magazine, 39–40
Murthy, Pratibha, rape and murder of, 51, 52–53, 54, 81–82, 83, 92–94, 93
mythology of rape and sexual violence, 15–17, 34, 35–40. *See also* stereotypes

Nagar, I., 17–18
naming and shaming of perpetrators, 8–9, 49, 70–72
Nandi, J., 51
Narayan, U., 32
National Crime Records Bureau (NCRB), 57–58, 101–102
Neuman, R. W., 62–63
news industry, Indian, 20–22
newspapers, 4–5, 17–18, 20–22, 61–62, 91, 112
newsrooms: in agenda-building, 24–25, 112–113; in feminist media theories, 29, 30–31, 35; in framing of rape, 14–15, 29, 35–36, 38–42; gatekeeping by, 109–110; male centricity of, 6, 36; patriarchy in, 17, 18; sexual harassment in, 57, 103–106, 111–112; social media's influence in, 48, 94
newsworthiness, 5–6, 14–15, 35–36, 37–39, 50
NGOs (nongovernmental organizations), 9, 14
Nguyen, A., 62
Nirbhaya movement/#Nirbhaya, 25, 44, 51, 84, 90–91, 91, 117n2. *See also* Singh, Jyoti, gang-rape and murder of
nonprofits, Indian, 44–45, 49, 50
Noopur (Smashboard), 48, 50, 54, 55

objectification of women's bodies, 5–6, 37–38, 40
objectivity, 18, 26, 31, 38
Occupy movement, 65–66
O'Hara, S., 17, 36
oppression of women, 26–27, 29–31, 36–37, 56
outrage, selective: in activism, 46–58; in agenda-building, 101, 102; in commentary on Facebook pages, 79; gatekeeping in, 54–55, 72–73; in hashtag movements, 70, 85, 86, 88, 89, 92–93, 95; in the Indian feminist movement, 14; marginalization in, 19–20; in the Suryanelli rape case, 100. *See also* biases

140 Index

Pariser, Eli, 99
Park street rape, 5–6, 56
passive voice in framing of rape, 16–17
Patekar, Nana, 90, 98
Patra, Reshma, 106–107
patriarchy, 5–6, 16–17, 18, 29–30, 32, 36, 37–39, 46–47
PERIO (GWU), 89
perpetrators: in acid attacks against victims, 95–96; activism in identification and arrest of, 102–103, 107–108; burden of proof for, 118n4; calls for revenge against, 43–44; in framing of rape, 14–15, 16–17, 18, 35–36, 38; in hashtag movements, 88–89, 90, 92, 94; in Jyoti Singh's rape and murder, 83–84; naming and shaming of, 8–9, 49, 70–72; normalization of, 111–112; in politicization, 56–57, 87
perspective, 16–17, 18–19, 29, 30–32, 33–34, 36, 38–39, 45
Peterson, K., 65–66
pitfalls of social media activism, 98–101
police: apathy of, in reporting and filing, 10, 86, 87; brutality by, 34, 61; inaction by, 89, 101–103; mainstream media coverage in action by, 107–108; rape and sexual harassment by, 3–4, 118n4; selective outrage by, 52. See also law enforcement
policy, public, 5, 20, 42–43, 92, 94, 99–100, 101–102, 112. See also law, Indian
policy makers, 52, 64, 95–96, 108–109
political party affiliation, 8–9, 13
politicians, 45, 86, 87, 92, 93–94, 95–96, 102–103
politicization of rape, 56–57, 87, 93–94, 96
politics, 14–15, 17–19, 35–36, 41, 46–47, 56–57, 70–73
power, 8, 15, 26, 41, 58, 72, 73
Pratap, journalist, 55, 96
print media, 4–5, 17–18, 20–22, 37–38, 59–60, 61–62, 91
privacy, 11–12, 85
protests: acid attacks in, 46–47; in agenda-setting, 84–86; in digital activism, 35; in framing of rape, 14–15, 17–18; grassroots, 13; hybrid, 42–44, 113; of Jyoti Singh's death, 52, 84–85; of the Mathura rape acquittal, 118n4; in the media landscape, 3, 6; selective outrage in, 53–54, 56; of the Unnao rape case, 86. See also hashtag movements, transnational

pseudonymous accounts, 108
punishment, 43–44, 46–47, 57, 81, 84–85

Quint, The, 97–98

race, 31–33, 36–37, 50. *See also* marginalization/marginalized groups
radical feminism, 29–31
Ragas, M. W., 61–62
Rakow, L., 30–31
Ramani, Priya, 111–112
Rao, 26, 40
rape: capitals of, 51–52; culture of, 90; in Indian law, 3–4, 99–100; mythology of, 15–17, 34, 35–40; as political issue, 24, 56–57; reporting of and convictions for, 57–58. *See also* framing of rape in the news media; gang rapes
rape script approach, 26–40
reception, 28–29, 38, 65
Red Brigade, 95
redressal system in the Indian news industry, 21–22
religion, 14, 50
repercussions for reporting, 46–47, 72–73, 90, 95–96
reporting/underreporting: in agenda-building, *101*, 101–102; compared to convictions, 57–58; discrimination in, 87–88; gap in, for rape, 110; of rapes of minority women, 16, 36–37; repercussions for, 46–47, 72–73, 90, 95–96
representation, 5, 17, 18–19, 27, 28–29, 40, 41–42
research institutes, women's, 13–14
responsibility, women's, 18, 26, 36, 41–42, 112
retaliation, rape as, in framing, 16–17
revenge, 36, 43–44, 81
reverse agenda-setting, 62–63
Rodgers, K., 14–15, 16–17, 35–36, 40–41
Ross, K., 29
Roy, Srila, 14, 71
rural activists/activism, 44–45, 49–50, 68, 72–73, 87, 89, 95, 113
rural/urban divide: algorithms in, 100–101; in framing of rape, 23–25, 44–45; in hashtag movements, 68–69, 70–71, 72–73, 86–89, 90, 92, 94–95; in journalism and activism, 23–24; in news coverage, 17, 87–88; in selective outrage, 48, 49–54, 88. *See also* location

safety, urban, 6, 18, 37–38, 51–52, 53–54, 83
Sandhya, activist, 46, 48
Sandip, journalist, 47
Sanjali rape and murder case, 100
Sanjib, journalist, 96
Sarkar, Raya, 23, 70
Sarkeesian, Anita, 34
"Savarna" feminism, 14. *See also* caste
Sayantanee, journalist and activist, 47, 55
#SayHerName, 34, 61
Sayre, B., 63
scandal, 48–49, 87–88. *See also* sensationalism
scripting rape and sexual assault, 26–40, 41–42
second-wave feminism, 3, 27–28
Seefelt, J. L., 37
self-care, 26
Sen, A., 40
sender-receiver model, 28–29
Sen-gupta, Reema, 106–107
Sengupta, S., 33
Sengupta, Ushoshi, 107–108
sensationalism, 5–6, 37–38, 110–111. *See also* scandal
sensitivity/insensitivity, gendered, 41–42
Seth, Leila, 85
sexism, 27, 28, 36–37, 58
sexual assault: fear of, 1; framing of, 24, 35–36, 40–42; as intimidation, 56–57; rape script approach to, 26–40. *See also* rape
sexual harassment: in academia, 23, 58, 70–72; agenda building on, 24–25, 43, 101–103; coverage of, 14–15, 17–18, 112–113; in the entertainment industry, 108–109; fear of, 1; in feminist methodology, 6–7; in Indian law, 3–4, 99–100; in the media workplace, 104–107; normalization of, 90–91; as political issue, 24, 56–57; reporting of and convictions for, 57–58; selective outrage on, 47–48, 49, 51, 53–54, 55–58; underreporting of, 10
sexuality, 14, 32–33
sexualization of victims, 16, 17, 35–36, 40
Shah, A.H., 48, 50
Shah, C., 63
Shah, D., 63
shaming of victims, 19–20, 26, 41–42
Shinde, Sushil Kumar, 52
Shome, R., 32–33
Sikanku, G., 60

Sikdar, Sanjay, 103–104
silos, 99–102
Singer, J., 109–110
Singh, Jyoti, gang-rape and murder of: brutality of, 5–6, 25, 37–38, 81, 83–84; framing of, 17–18, 35; in hashtag movements, 43–44, 76–77, 78–81, 83–85, 93, 94; identification in press coverage of, 82, 83; in increase in filed complaints, 101–102; selective outrage on, 51, 53; sensationalization of, 5–6, 37–38; as turning point, 4, 81, 83–85, 99–100
Sircar, O., 44
Smashboard, 48
socialist feminism, 29–31
spaces, public, 17, 26, 41, 53–54, 56, 72–73
spatial politics in framing of rape, 35–36, 41
Steeves, H., 29–30
Steiner, Linda, 31–32
stereotypes, 15–16, 27, 28–29, 38–39, 47. *See also* mythology of rape and sexual violence
stigmatization, 5–6, 10, 16, 17, 37–38, 40
street harassment, 1, 43, 79, 102–103
structure/structural issues, 13, 15, 35–36, 41–42, 82, 111, 112
Subhro, journalist, 54, 82
Subramanium, Gopal, 85
suicide, 88, 89
superficiality of social media activism, 99
Suryanelli rape case, 48–49, 100
sustainability in hashtag movements, 68–69, 90–91
Sutapa, activist, 2, 46, 50, 72–73

Tarun, journalist, 55
television news and media, 20–21, 59–60, 61–62, 94–95
Tewksbury, D., 60
Thakuri, Pradeep: "5 Years on, It's the Same Ordeal for Nirbhayas," 99–100
#thelist, 72–73
themes in news coverage of rapes, 92–93, 93
third-wave feminism, 6–7, 27, 33–34
threats, 45, 46–47, 79, 83–84, 86
Times of India, 53, 53–54
Tiwari, Prashanti, 57
transnational feminism, 31, 32–36, 39–40, 42, 66–68, 70–73
trivialization of women, 27

TVF (The Viral Fever production company), 106–107

21st Century India, "Against Rape," 74, 80–81

Twitter: in agenda-building/setting, 62–63, 73, 84–85, 89, 102, 106–107, 109–110; concerns of activists about, 98–99; in feminist theorization and digital activism, 34; harassment and abuse on, 2–3; personal experiences on, 46; selective outrage on, 44–45, 49–50

Twohey, M., 111

Tyagi, Maya, 3

Unnao rape case, 82, 86, 88, 92, 93

Uttar Pradesh, 86, 95–96, 100

Vandello, J. A., 37

Verma, J.S., 84–85

"victim," use of, as ethical challenge, 11

victims: blaming of, 1, 10–11, 15–16, 36–37, 38–39, 47–48, 102–103; challenges faced by, 99–100; doubting of, 19–20, 90, 106–107; in framing of rape, 14–17, 18, 19–20, 35–39, 40; global similarities in treatment of, 2; honor of, 5–6, 18, 26, 37–38; identification of, 10, 82–83, 94; valuation of, 93–94

virality of the #MeToo movement, 89

virginity tests, 85

virgin/whore dichotomy, 15–16

Visakha Guidelines for sexual harassment policies at work, 3–4

visibility, 16–17, 50, 90–91

voluntary feminist organizations, 14

vulnerability of women, 2–3, 15–16, 73, 87, 92

Wasnik, Chaitali, sexual harassment of, 102

websites, news, 24, 60–61, 73, 75, 76, 78, 79, 94, 106–107

Weinbaum, A., et al: *The Modern Girl Around the World*, 41

Weinstein, Harvey, 90, 111

West, Lindy: "I Quit Twitter and It Feels Great," 98–99

Western, M., 62

Western media, 32–33

WhatsApp, 45, 50, 98

Winfrey, Oprah, 113

Wire, The, 97–98

wire services in agenda setting, 59–60

women of color. *See* marginalization/marginalized groups

women's cells, 47

women's groups, autonomous, 13

workplace harassment, 3–4, 83, 90–91, 104–107, 111–113. *See also* newsrooms

worthiness/unworthiness in framing of rape, 14–15, 35–36

Worthington, N., 16, 18, 36, 38

Yamaguchi, T., 41

ABOUT THE AUTHOR

PALLAVI GUHA is an assistant professor of journalism at Towson University and a former journalist. Her research includes anti-rape and anti-sexual harassment activism on mass media and social media platforms. She has a PhD in journalism from the University of Maryland, and her academic background lies in the intersection of political science, international relations, journalism, and women's studies.